A creative tension

Edited by Anja Meulenbelt, Joyce Outshoorn,
Selma Sevenhuijsen and Petra de Vries

A creative tension

Key Issues of Socialist-Feminism

translated by Della Couling

South End Press

Boston

The articles in this book first appeared in the *Socialisties-Feministiese Teksten* anthologies, published in Holland between 1980 and 1983.
English edition and compilation first published in 1984 in the United States of America by South End Press, 302 Columbus Avenue, Boston, MA 02116

Cover designed by Bonnie Acker

Phototypeset by A.K.M. Associates (UK) Ltd., Ajmal House,
Hayes Road, Southall, Greater London
Printed in Great Britain by Photobooks (Bristol) Limited
Bound by W.H. Ware & Sons Limited,
Tweed Road, Clevedon, Avon

ISBN 0-89608-236-9

Contents

Introduction / 1

1. The women's movement and motherhood
   Selma Sevenhuijsen and Petra de Vries / 9

2. Domestic and public *Marijke Mossink* / 26

3. The dual heritage *Joyce Outshoorn* / 43

4. Feminism and psychoanalysis *Aafke Komter* / 60

5. 'The Policing of Families' *Selma Sevenhuijsen and Jolande Withuis* / 85

6. Women's struggles in the Third World
   Annemiek Hoogenboom and Annemieke Voets / 103

Notes / 130

Introduction

This book is a selection of essays which originally appeared as articles in the Netherlands in *Socialist Feminist Texts (Socialisties-Feministiese Teksten)*. The *Texts* are anthologies about the theory and practice of the women's movement. Seven issues have appeared since 1977, all edited by our collective: Anja Meulenbelt, Joyce Outshoorn, Selma Sevenhuijsen and Petra de Vries. We were all active in the feminist movement in the Netherlands at the beginning, then in consciousness raising (CR) groups (which became the backbone of feminism here), and in the Feminist Socialist Platform, a group which evolved during the seventies in an attempt to unite all left wing feminists, whether aligned or non-aligned. We have also worked in the abortion campaign, in the trade unions and in the feminist media as well as taking part in the fight over the right of parental access to children after divorce, in setting up women's studies and in feminist community and social work.

There is a strong women's movement in the Netherlands. In the 15 years since it began, feminism has influenced the ideas of many women and men about the relationship between the sexes. Its impact is felt in politics at a national level, in party politics, social work, health and education, and in science. The movement is countrywide, so even small towns often have a women's centre, a women's cafe or an active group of feminists. The number of people involved in a movement does not necessarily equal its effectiveness, nevertheless it is impressive that the woman's diary now sells 80,000 copies a year. At least that many women feel confident enough to declare their sympathy with the women's movement. We can distinguish four main areas in which feminists work and organize. These are feminist culture, women's aid, adult education for women and working as feminists within left wing organizations.

Feminist 'culture' consists of theatre groups, magazines, newsletters, TV programmes, bookshops and the creation of comfortable places for women to relax in such as restaurants, cafes, dances and festivals. Why should women wait till after the revolution to have fun? Cultural activities create a 'way in' for women not familiar with the movement. Women soon leave the movement if there is no fun, and social activities provide an opportunity for window shopping before deciding on the level of commitment a woman wants to make.

Many women are involved in some form of women's aid or feminist support. This work is comparable to that in other countries. We have battered women's shelters, rape crisis centres, health centres and feminist therapy institutions. The aims and ideas of these projects do not differ basically from those abroad, but there is a difference in their funding. Our central and local governments have given financial support to these and other feminist initiatives. On the one hand this meant valuable support, on the other hand state funding created considerable tension and discussion around such questions as how much influence the state would get, what would happen if they stopped their funding and developed a policy of making women voluntary social workers (which they did), how to cope when some women on a project are paid wages while others work voluntarily, what strategy to develop if some projects in one field are subsidized and others are not. Many of these questions were solved at a practical level, either by saying 'we need the money' or 'it's not worth ending up with a very small grant if we have to travel through the bureaucracy to get it'. Yet the theoretical question of the relationship between the state and feminism remains. There is a contradiction because we want the state to provide good services while at the same time many feminists distrust state politics and do not want to be controlled.

Two areas of feminist work have had particular influence on our movement. One is the feminist involvement in adult education for women, the other is feminist work within left wing organizations.

Many feminists want to extend the movement to involve poor and working-class women. This has resulted in a vast network of courses for women with only primary and some secondary education. Adult education or 'second chance education' is often the first chance women get to study something they like. Groups exist in community centres, at adult education institutes or as autonomous feminist projects, either local government sponsored or self-supporting. The specific contents of courses differ, depending on the students and on the women who teach them. The teachers are often students in feminist social work or university students. Some groups are like CR groups, others study an academic subject (biology, arithmetic), yet others have a more practical purpose, such as learning to read newspapers.

In the 1970s the adult education network grew rapidly, courses became widespread and at times very popular. Feminism could develop in this way because of the specific situation of women in the Netherlands. It is one of the countries with the lowest percentage of women in the labour force in the western world. Most women are housewives who only come into contact with feminism through activities that are located close to *their* workplace (the home) and fit in with their needs. There are feminist trade union courses but they only appeal to a few of those interested in feminism. Women have a variety of reasons for wanting to learn: in order to be able 'to help children with their homework', to compensate for their lack of education, 'because it is interesting' or, 'because it's nice to be out of the house sometimes'.

It hasn't always been easy to keep courses under feminist control. Sometimes local authorities demand that all women's organizations including Catholic and Protestant ones have a say in course content and appointing teaching staff. Sometimes a left wing group may see the courses as an opportunity 'to mobilize housewives'.

For these reasons, the courses are not often advertised as feminist, nor do the contents always refer to women's movement issues. Nevertheless the existence of the feminist adult education network has broadened the social base of the movement. Women got together with others in similar situations and often moved from the development of their personal consciousness to a genuine interest in feminism. It must be added, however, that few black or working-class women hold positions in the movement, or influence its politics and strategy.

In recent years the feminist network in adult education has changed. There are fewer courses independent of other institutions and attendances are down. It may well be that courses inevitably fare better when supported by existing organizations such as community centres. And there is a limit to what can be offered year after year in a course. Women obviously won't take the same course again and again. The economic crisis is often given as an explanation for everything, yet it may have influenced women's wish to change themselves, as well as causing a reduction in the number of courses offered.

Feminism had an impact not only on women but also on political parties, left and right, as well as on government and its policies. It was satisfying to hear a male TV newsreader presenting official state policy about putting an end to sexual violence, and to hear these feminist ideas enter the living rooms of millions of people. It is important as a symbol. It shows that the state now takes our demands seriously and no longer sees women's liberation as something only concerned with discrimination at work and who's doing the dishes.

We can also see that feminists have influenced the policies of political parties and trade unions. This includes such statements as the 'recognition of domestic and voluntary work as productive and valuable labour in society' (Labour Party) or 'care for children and housework is a joint responsibility of husband and wife' (Federation of Dutch Trade Unions) or 'fighting the system of compulsory heterosexuality should be one of our first priorities' (Pacifist Socialist Party).

It seems feminists have won some battles. So how and why did socialist feminism develop in the Netherlands and how did such feminism relate to the non feminist left?

In 1969 the birth of the modern women's movement witnessed the revival of an old style 'socialist feminism' in the formation of an autonomous group called Dolle Mina. Dolle Mina was composed of women and men from a variety of left backgrounds.

In a short time it attracted thousands of other women. Dolle Mina's idea of socialism was the 'shoulder to shoulder' kind: organize shoulder to shoulder with working class men in order to seize the means of production, with women entering the labour market in order to be truly liberated. This strategy was based on classic and often criticized marxist analysis: women's oppression is caused by class divisions, private property and capitalism; it is an abstract ideological phenomenon, not an immediate issue.

With hindsight we can write ironically about the period when 'socialism' and/or 'feminism' was such a crucial debate. But it was necessary to deal with the left legacy of the sixties. The idea that women's economic vulnerability was the key problem (and still is) was not exclusive to the socialists in Dolle Mina but was also held by the much less radical Man Vrouw Maatschappij (Man-Woman Society – MVM) an organization that saw itself as a pressure group within traditional political parties.

It took three years before such concepts as sexism, patriarchy, and reproduction opened up ways of asking new theoretical questions. In the meantime it became painfully clear that classical marxism could not solve the problems of domestic labour, love, sexual violence and women's lack of political power. The realization came when women who were frustrated with MVM and Dolle Mina formed consciousness raising groups. These spread rapidly and created a strong basis for the development of the movement. After that, in 1973, socialist feminism entered a new stage when the need arose to connect the experiences of consciousness raising with a more theoretical analysis of women's position in society. In 1975 a 'Feminist Socialist Platform' was founded to unite all left feminists, whether aligned or non-aligned. The feminist socialist current regarded itself as part of the autonomous women's movement and a base where women could get the support for feminist struggles in their workplaces and in left parties and groups. The importance of organizing as feminists in parties and other institutions was stressed from the very beginning. The Platform was a loose network for keeping in touch and exchanging experiences. Since the platform included women from a wide political spectrum (from Communist Party to Social Democrat as well as women from the smaller 'vanguards of the working class'), its socialism was eclectic and not confined to any one theory or strategy.

While the 'socialism' of feminist socialism was broadly defined, its feminism was rooted firmly in CR. It was possible for large numbers of women to identify with it and for a long time it seemed that feminist socialism was the only significant current in Dutch feminism.

After 1974 feminist activity grew in the four left wing political parties as well as in the trade unions, especially the teachers' union and the civil servants' union. During this period we started our attack on institutions such as schools, universities and social work.

We encountered many problems on many levels in particular the culture of the left, its organizational structure and its theories. Strategies and theories on the left fit male workers. They are often modelled on images of workers who account for only a small part of the total labour force. The images are of masculine, proletarian and unskilled factory workers. In addition, feminists working in parties and unions have to communicate their ideas and demands in a language that is understood by party officials. This often means talking in terms that do not fit our ideas very well. How do you speak of the sexual harassment of women at work in the language of collective bargaining?

There is also the problem of male bureaucratic structures which make it difficult to form small women's groups. Small groups are seen by those on the outside as just a remedy for 'women who are scared in big meetings' not as a necessary means for finding out what our work problems are and how to formulate our demands. Small groups are given no formal status whatsoever in big structures.

Some women ascend through the male hierarchy because, if you have argued for years that more women should get leadership positions, it is difficult to refuse one when it is offered. Then women at the top get isolated from those at the bottom.

It is difficult to assess how much influence feminists have had on the left, but it is certainly true that the women's liberation movement has political weight. No-one anymore openly dares to question the importance of the feminist cause. Our power, however, is limited. Even if the left was on the feminist side in all issues, which certainly isn't the case, feminists in parties and unions often complain how rarely good intentions are put into practice.

The move into institutions and parties reduced the need for a separate socialist feminist platform. The Platform and local feminist socialist study groups formally dissolved in 1979 but since the feminist socialist movement was not only an organization but also an idea, the idea of socialist feminism did not disappear with the dissolution of the Platform. Many socialist feminists are still actively fighting in parties and unions, in fields like health and education, and in campaigns such as the campaign for economic independence of women and the abortion campaign. Ideas which first originated in the feminist socialist current have become common to all feminists. These include an understanding of the importance of domestic labour, the effects of state policy on women and sexual divisions at work.

Recently the meaning of socialist feminism has changed. A socialist feminist magazine has dropped 'socialist' from its title and many left women identify with feminism over socialism. The meaning of the term 'autonomous' has also changed. It used to refer to the independence of feminism from left organizations and their leadership. It meant women's independence from men and making our own analysis of our oppression. Now 'autonomous' means having a non-funded, self-supporting feminist project with no ties to other institutions. It also means 'non-reformist' or rejecting parliamentarianism.

The *Socialist Feminist Texts* grew out of the socialist feminist current and are part of it. We called ourselves not feminist socialists but socialist feminists, to show that we identified first and foremost with feminism and the women's movement. We also called ourselves socialist because we inherited ideas from marxism, specifically a historical materialist view. This means that we assume that ideas, including feminist ones, relate to the material and historical conditions of people's lives and that those conditions are defined largely by capitalist relations as well as patriarchal ones. We committed ourselves to writing theoretical material in order to stimulate the discussion on feminism and socialism, to show how complex the position of women is and to draw on various disciplines to demonstrate this. Just as the scope of feminist socialism was wide, so was ours. Our feminism has always been radical with a strong emphasis on the importance of the personal as political and on matters not raised by the traditional left, such as sexuality and 'body-politics'.

After our experiences with the intellectual left, we developed a suspicion of the academic debates of some marxists. We wished to preserve a link with the active politics of the women's movement which led us to a policy of selecting articles on current debates, commissioning articles on the politics of the movement, always asking women involved in activity to write and asking our more academic writers to put their articles into a practical political perspective.

Subjects covered by articles in the *Texts* include sexuality racism, labour market theories and women and the state. We also introduced Dutch readers to the work of Gayle Rubin, Adrienne Rich and Linda Gordon. In selecting articles for *A Creative Tension*, we have neglected articles with a purely Dutch focus and chosen those with a more international dimension.

Amsterdam, Febuary 1984
Anja Meulenbelt, Joyce Outshoorn,
Selma Sevenhuijsen and Petra de Vries

1. The women's movement and motherhood

Selma Sevenhuijsen and Petra de Vries

Introduction

Nearly all women are faced at some time with the dilemma of whether or not to have children. Every woman as a daughter experiences her relationship with her mother, a complex one in our culture. Every woman is faced by the expectation that she will become a mother. Many women will at some time experience the fear of an unwanted pregnancy. Many women become mothers without having chosen to do so. Women who are mothers experience the complex pressures which motherhood entails under present-day social conditions.

The women's movement has after years of apparent relative calm, suddenly acquired an interest in the problems associated with motherhood. The swelling flood of publications in this field is the most visible sign of this. The writers of this essay are following the current debate on motherhood. We have long intended to write on the subject. We have both been concerned for some years about motherhood, as a result of our experiences as mother and non-mother. We have studied the way in which people in the women's movement think about women with children. We also both work as researchers into aspects of motherhood.

Discussions on motherhood and the women's movement in the editorial offices of the *Texts* led us to the idea of running a series of articles on various aspects of motherhood. We wanted to begin with an article outlining the problem. This 'introduction to a series' grew progressively longer and became less of an introduction and more an article in its own right. Nevertheless, we would still like to regard the following as an introductory account, an exploration of the relationship between the women's movement and motherhood.

In the first part of this essay we analyze the ideas about motherhood which dominated the thinking of feminists in the first years of the present wave of feminism. Contemporary feminism was at first characterized by a powerful resistance to traditional ideas about motherhood.[1] This resistance was necessary for the development of a radically new outlook on motherhood, but it also had drawbacks. We threw the baby out with the bathwater when we rejected existing images of motherhood. In the second part of this essay, we investigate the positive and negative effects of this.

We would like to see a new feminist definition of motherhood. We conclude our essay with some pointers toward this. Changing ideas of motherhood have consequences for the theory and strategy of the women's movement. We confine ourselves to three areas: childcare, fatherhood and reproduction. The material we have used for this essay is taken from our own memories, other women's accounts, women's movement journals, theoretical literature on motherhood and extracts from historical writings of the contemporary women's movement.[2]

> I have something against the ideology that demands of all women that they become mothers, and against the circumstances under which women are mothers. At present motherhood is for women a trap and for that reason I would advise women not to be mothers.[3]

Simone de Beauvoir's statement was not sensational although more weight is ascribed to her words than to those of just any feminist. Feminists have long opposed the idea that motherhood is the only destiny for women. In the first years of the contemporary women's movement, it was still necessary to argue what has since become feminist common knowledge. Then it was revolutionary to criticize the idea that all children need their mothers twenty-four hours a day, to say that the maternal instinct in women is not inborn, that men are also capable of looking after children well. The dominant ideology of motherhood was exhaustively criticized, the criticism concentrating mainly on the supposed link between biological and social motherhood.

Feminist criticism of motherhood emphasized the tedious sides of motherhood. Traditional ideas about motherhood stressed beauty, love, devotion and satisfaction. Feminists on the other hand emphasized guilt feelings, self-sacrifice, self-denial and thanklessness. They described how motherhood could become a miserable trap. This emerged in the *Moederboek* (Mother Book) published in Holland in 1976. It contained women's accounts of how dismal and frustrating motherhood could be, interspersed with short theoretical pieces. Motherhood was characterized by the key words: frustration, guilt feelings and monstrosity. The book could usefully have carried a separate supplement saying 'This book is a final warning. Don't do it. Motherhood is dangerous for women.'[4]

The attack on existing ideas about motherhood meant that children were not welcome in some sections of the women's movement. Childcare was seldom or never thought about either in meetings or in our activity. It was regarded exclusively as the responsibility of mothers. If childcare was ever thought about then it resulted merely in the provision of a little room for the children and a woman who did want to take care of them. No-one understood that childcare could mean organizing interesting activities for children. Many mothers in the women's movement have experienced the movement's hostility to children, which was also expressed in a lack of understanding, or even criticism, of pregnant women. Motherhood was a 'political' problem in theory, but in reality it remained a domestic matter.

From the outset the women's movement, or rather women within the women's movement, adopted a negative attitude to motherhood. Liberation was regarded as liberation from the duty to become a mother. Freedom was the 'freedom' to opt against motherhood. So we fought for the right to abortion but few defended the right to pregnancy.

With hindsight it is remarkable that large groups of women could so easily free themselves of the traditional image of women. That this also determined the image of feminism is accounted for by the fact that the second feminist wave was initially more a movement of daughters than of mothers. The first feminist attempts at forming a theory were also affected by this. Shulamith Firestone's *The Dialectic of Sex*[5] provides a good example. Ten years ago Firestone's ideas seemed shocking, especially to women of the left. In her view sexual class not economic class forms the basis for the oppression of women. She explains that the sexual class system is based on biological inequality between women and men. Women bear and suckle children which gives rise to a division of labour oppressive for women. Firestone's ideas about the conditions for women's liberation follow logically from her theoretical position. For her one of the most important pre-conditions for liberation is the liberation of women from the tyranny of reproductive biology, using every means possible. 'Every means possible' includes artificial reproduction via test tubes, a view often seriously advocated by travelling American feminists of the early women's movement.

Many of Firestone's ideas were swamped by indignant reactions to her thoughts on test tube babies and loud criticism of the ahistorical analysis on which her ideas on biology and technology are based.[6] Apart from this indignation over her belief in the technological revolution, Firestone's message that having children is in itself oppressive, corresponded with women's liberation ideas prevalent here at the time.

If we look at the first demands and activities to emerge from the women's movement, motherhood appears not to have been very important. We were concerned mainly with work outside the home, sexuality, abortion, sex roles and training and education. But a closer look reveals that a particular idea of motherhood provided the basis for many of our demands and activities. Sometimes motherhood was a central theme. This becomes clearer if we see our demands in the light of the above-mentioned negative attitude towards motherhood. The theoretical analysis at the start of the women's movement was, in so far as it existed, that women's oppression is the result of the economic dependence of women, and is maintained by the obstacles that prevent women from going out to work.[7] We tried to solve this through demands for the extension of pregnancy leave, free crèches, part-time work, a more equal division of labour in the home and play centres for schoolchildren. All these demands were aimed at obtaining for mothers a position equal to that of men in the labour market.

There is nothing wrong with these demands – they have yet to be granted and we shall still have to fight for them. But what we want to show here is that they saw women simply from a male viewpoint. They stressed only what women don't do – work outside the home. They assumed that feminism is the desire to be equal to men. We completely ignored women's work as mothers.

Because the emphasis always lay on demands which centred on women's role as workers, it appeared that the central problems of motherhood were in the area of time-tabling, and that better services and the right to work outside the home were 'solutions' for the motherhood problem.

At the beginning of the women's movement the motherhood problem was defined as follows:

(1) Motherhood is a restriction on working outside the home.

(2) Children are a hindrance in attempts by women to achieve an equal position with men, they are a nuisance and demand all your attention.

(3) Looking after children is an attack on your own identity.

(4) For feminists the political problem is whether or not to have children.

This 'old definition' still has an influence on feminist thought. It is therefore important to examine both its positive and negative sides.

The women's movement grew up at a time when women in the Netherlands rarely worked outside the home if it was not economically necessary. Equally it was unheard of even to think about 'strangers' looking after your children. Women with children had to, and still do, move heaven and earth to be able to work outside the home and also struggle with their guilt feelings if they take their children to a crèche.

For many women with children getting to know other mothers in the women's movement brought an enormous relief. Just to be able to say 'I'm not a good mother' or 'I sometimes feel like throwing the kids over the balcony' is liberating if all you have ever heard is that mothers naturally always love their children.

For women who had no children the rejection of the traditional idea of motherhood was an important element in the construction of a feminist identity. To break out of the limits society set for women meant an automatic break with what was defined as feminine. If you became a feminist that usually meant a rejection of the traditional manner of female fulfilment – motherhood. Simone de Beauvoir's advice did not fall on deaf ears. For some women the choice of whether or not to be a mother became almost a question of feminist conscience.

These new attitudes were a necessary step in dealing with sexist ideology. In order for women to develop new images and ideas on motherhood, they had to break with what had always been represented as their destiny. As motherhood was junked the rest of the package – motherhood–marriage–heterosexuality – was also thrown overboard.

The 'old definition' of the motherhood problem has a number of shortcomings. The problem of whether or not to have children was (and is) important for young women without children. This meant that for feminists the problem of motherhood appeared to be reduced to a problem of choice.[8] There are two difficulties with this view. First, 'choice' is just as misleading a word as 'chance' or 'possibility'. They are words that obscure the fact that the problems involved are not individual but collective political problems. Choice presupposes an activity belonging to the individual and if she has made the 'wrong choice', then she can only reproach herself. Women are forced to make a choice, because motherhood, unlike fatherhood, given the present-day division of labour, is difficult to combine with other activities. Many women have pointed out that the 'decision' about children is made in an ambivalent way – 'the right of self-determination cannot exist if none of the alternatives looks attractive.'[9] When people are asked whether their children were planned, their replies are often ambiguous: 'yes, they were planned, but . . .'[10] There is no real choice.[11] For individual women there still remains a huge problem, but the political strategy should be directed at changing the circumstances that force women to a choice.

So long as motherhood is talked of in the women's movement as a choice for or against, a trap or otherwise, there will be little scope for women's own concerns. Non-mothers find it difficult to clarify their wishes, doubts and ambivalences concerning motherhood. Mothers cannot talk about their concrete experiences as mother, about the pleasant sides of being a mother and about their own problems.

In 1973 a woman remarked that the attitude to motherhood in the women's movement was too one-sided: 'Any kind of warm relationship with your children is interpreted as being on your knees before the holy motherhood of former generations, ideologically forbidden and jeered at.'[12] And today we still often find that feminists who talk about the pleasant sides of motherhood are immediately told that they are playing into the hands of the 'right' or are even inventing a 'new ideology of motherhood'. It still happens that defensive attitudes prevail, when the issue is presented as a 'choice'.

Monika Jaeckel and Greta Tüllmann rightly point out that a great deal of our energy goes into a distinction between mothers and non-mothers, to prove who has the best solution to dilemmas we have not brought upon ourselves.[13]

Another negative effect of the 'old definition' of motherhood is that it kept a number of women's problems invisible, both in the theory and in the practice of feminism. If we look at society from the viewpoint of women with children there are many areas where feminist politics have still to be developed. The relationship between women and children is one. Society is extremely hostile to children. This is concealed by the fact that women are made responsible for the protection of children. It is no accident that women and children are lumped together. Children are also oppressed by patriarchal attitudes.[14] This shows itself in their total absence from public life. They are not tolerated in cafes, restaurants, public meetings. They cannot move away from their mothers, or they will be run over by a car. They cannot arrange their relations with other children and adults independently, because traffic and modern forms of living isolate people from one another. They are bound to their mothers and vice versa.

We need a feminist view of the place and importance of children in the 'domestic sphere'. The feminist ideal of liberation would then be seen in a different light. In the beginning we were so keen to escape from being isolated housewives that we failed to see that this would limit our relations with children to the sort of relations that men have with them: a quick kiss before going to bed and a trip to the zoo on Sundays. Women don't want to be shut up all day with children, but the alternative is not carrying out alienated work or making a career in the men's world. The politicization of the domestic sphere means assessing the true worth of relations between people, including those between women and children.

In the early theory of the women's movement motherhood remained largely invisible. It appeared in the debate on domestic work only as the means of producing future generations. The rearing of children was put on the same level as washing up and making the beds. So it has never become clear why women do housework, or how important they are to capital in reproducing other people.[15] Motherhood has also been absent in feminist theory on families. In the last decade it has become clear that the family was not the gender-neutral alliance of the sociology books. The discovery that women and men fight out the battle between the sexes inside families and that power and violence exist in the family was important. The family reflects power relations in the outside world.[16] Children as well as men and women live in families. They are the power structures which determine the conditions for women's mothering.

Recently the interest in motherhood has grown in the women's movement. This is in part due to there being more mothers in the movement. Feminism has reached women who already had children before they came into contact with the women's movement, and many of the young feminists who hesitated for years about whether to have a child have now become mothers. Since we separated out the package of marriage–family–motherhood–heterosexuality, it has also become attractive to have a child. In a few years BOM women (Bewust Ongehuwde Moeders or Deliberately Unmarried Mothers) have become almost a national institution in the Netherlands.

One reason for the popularity of motherhood is that our experiences in the abortion campaign and setting up better life and health care have taught us that control over women's ability to have children plays a central role in their oppression.

The interest in motherhood is also connected with the search for the roots of our oppression in the mother-daughter relationship. This new interest will doubtless lead to a new theory and new attitudes to motherhood as motherhood becomes a central theme for feminists. This in turn will influence theory and strategy in the women's movement at large. We think that a new definition of motherhood should be based on an understanding that:

(i) Oppression is not caused by women bearing children, nor are children the source of their mothers' oppression. Motherhood is made unattractive by the relations in which women bear and bring up children.

(ii) Motherhood is an obstacle to working outside the home, but the opposite is also true. The way in which paid labour is organized makes it difficult for women to enjoy motherhood and remain independent.

(iii) Motherhood not only involves caring for and rearing children. Motherhood is also a special relationship between one or more adults and children, which like any relationship has pleasant and unpleasant sides. Motherhood is not only self-sacrifice, you also get something back. We have gradually been able to imagine motherhood free of the family and everything attached to it. We can now see the attractive sides of life with children more clearly.

(iv) Society cannot be really changed if we overlook how we reproduce ourselves. This means considering both biological motherhood and the upbringing of children. The strategy of refraining from child-bearing to bring patriarchy to its knees is, in our view, doomed to failure. It falls into the same trap as those who debate whether or not to have children. A feminist vision of the preservation of the species is better than a vision of its end.

This new definition has consequences for theoretical and strategic questions in the women's movement. Three examples make this clear.

If you say at feminist socialist meetings that motherhood is a political problem, people invariably reply: 'Yes, we all agree. There must be crèches.' Collectivization of domestic work recurs as a constant theme in the demands of the women's movement.[17] These include public laundries, crèches, daycare, collective eating-places and collective housing. The demands give the women's movement a socialist face, slotting into the tradition of the 'socialization of the means of production'. The demands are too glib. Children are something more than means of production or little lumps of labour force. We want to make a distinction between collectivizing motherhood and collectivizing domestic work. Different problems demand different solutions. Washing and cooking can be more efficient if socialized. Children can go to a crèche for part of the time. But efficiency is a rotten way to approach a relationship between people. There are limits to the collectivization of motherhood, which emerge in discussions of the demand for crèches, control over reproduction and looking after children.

The women's movement demanded crèches mainly because these enable women to work outside the home. We have learned since that crèches do not solve the problems of the double load. Working outside the home, rushing to the crèche and doing the shopping, remains a difficult combination. Mothers who work outside the home are under constant stress because of the absurd organization of labour in our society and its strict division along sex lines both inside and outside the home. Because mothering is often such an individualized activity the consequences of the division are constantly put on to individual women. You can't pretend your children don't exist up until the evening when it's time to collect them from the crèche on your way home. With older children the crèche is out of the question anyway. The problems of motherhood are not solved simply by providing enough crèches.

If the work which is at present organized around the male breadwinner, were adapted to mothers instead of the other way round, it would no longer be a question of more part time opportunities, and better social provision. The changes would have to go deeper. In the ideal feminist socialist society 'mothering' and work outside the home would be integrated in the lives of both women and men. That is why feminists entered the discussion on shortening working hours. A shorter working week brings an integrated society a little closer.

The demand for crèches is a political expression of the difficulties of mothering and working outside the home. Crèches are an important demand for the current women's movement. This was reflected in the recent demonstrations against the increase in parental contributions to daycare centres. But the women's movement could do more than make quantitative demands for childcare. The form and quality of collectivized childcare is of political importance too. If we want more 'state provisions' in daycare then who will decide about educational philosophy or training programmes? Under present conditions it is not impossible that mothers (and fathers) will be left out of decision making about, say, the relationships between girls and boys in a particular institution.

Many women anyway object to crèches and this is not simply because 'they can't see their own interests', as some in the women's movement would argue. A more likely explanation for the objections is that women don't want to lose control of the one area in which they still have some say – the care of children. Children are often the only people with whom women have a close emotional bond, in whom they find the warmth they do not get elsewhere.

We should also realize that there are forms of collectivized childcare other than crèches. Women arrange a great deal of 'invisible' daycare themselves: groups of mothers in neighbourhoods who take turns at home, grandmothers who look after small children, and collective forms of housing. In the women's movement too we have become involved in 'sharing' children, during holidays, or women without children take part of the responsibility for other women's children. These forms of collectivization are not geared to work outside the home, so much as they are concerned with breaking out of isolation, providing mutual support, solving problems of childrearing together and breaking out of the ideology of the unbreakable bond between mother and child. The ideal form of collectivization must cater for these needs as well as support working mothers.

When in 1970 the feminist movement revived, one of its first demands was that men should also care for children. Women had to have more opportunities for work outside the home, therefore men had to do their share of domestic work. And because we discovered that mothering is not a question of biology, it seemed obvious that men could do it just as well. The problem of fatherhood seemed to be solved. Reality wasn't that simple, and today we have little reason for optimism about the sharing of childcare between women and men. Women often have to put up a real fight in order to create equality in this area. It is still women who get up in the night to see to a crying baby, who stay home from work when a child is ill. Moreover, you can't force men to comfort a child.

Some individual men seriously work at a new kind of fatherhood. But they are still an exception and anyway, as Adrienne Rich said, they should not expect too much thankfulness and love: they should behave as our equals, without the need for any 'applause' for being special. There is certainly little evidence of a collective effort among men to rethink mothering, fatherhood and relations with children. There may be in the men's movement, but little has emerged so far. Men within the organizations such as trade unions and political parties still maintain the traditional ideal of masculinity. Left wing men always see the five hour working day as a women's matter, never as a progressive step for men. Men tend to see caring as detrimental to achievement, career and being the breadwinner.

Men in a patriarchal society are not qualified for motherhood and it is perhaps time that we demand they become qualified and that they work creatively towards being admitted to our territory. If we don't do so we risk losing the last bit of influence we have, without getting anything in return.[18]

The demands for equal division of tasks are real so long as we are dealing with heterosexuality, and using the family as point of departure. Many feminist women have broken away from lives with men and have no plans of ever again embarking on a heterosexual relationship. Women who criticize the oppressive behaviour of men, withdraw from it and share ever smaller parts of their life with them, do not want to share something as fundamental as child raising with them. And if women no longer want that then a new feminist strategy on fatherhood is needed. We are confronted with a difficult problem. If we opt for raising children independently of men, we may end up in the traditional positon that mothering is the special domain of women. If on the other hand we aim at a new kind of fatherhood, we risk making ourselves dependent on men again, in a different way.

Adrienne Rich states how important an emotional bond is between sons and 'mothering men' for breaking through the charged mother-son relationship in patriarchy and for creating a new sort of masculinity.[19] It is an important view, but the question is whether individual women have enough energy to get individual men to the point of being more than weekend fathers. To make demands for a new sort of fatherhood means that feminists must also investigate the ways in which men try to safeguard traditional fatherhood. Two areas deserve our attention, fathers' rights, and whether children need fathers.

Present developments indicate that groups of men use the law and therefore the power of the state to safeguard traditional paternal authority against independent motherhood. Until recently the authority of fathers was legally established in private and family law ('the man is the head of the matrimonial alliance').[20] The possibilities for divorce were limited. These regulations have been amended in favour of women during the past decade. Now that divorce legislation is being reviewed we see a boomerang effect. Men try to use the proposed new legal provisions to limit women's rights. Newspapers run pathetic tales about divorced fathers who are left out and publicize occupations of buildings by men who are demanding legally enforceable right of access to children after divorce.[21] It is striking that men in this situation appeal for 'equal rights' or 'the best interests of the child'. They don't want an equal right to the care of children, but rather a right to custody (in which care is frequently handed over to another woman) or a right to children as weekend pastime.

Psychologists always say that children, particularly boys, need fathers for identification. According to Freudian psychology boys identify with the traditional man/father role.[22] Legislators also use this argument in the question of access rights. We wish to reconsider this argument from a feminist view. We do not want our sons to identify with the traditional masculinity that we ourselves were oppressed by. It is anyway not clear whether boys need an identification figure. If they do, then why can't sons identify with strong mothers?

Discussions about motherhood bring us to the potential power women possess on the basis of their biological reproductive ability, and the way in which this power is oppressed and manipulated. There are few words and terms in which feminist questions about the reproduction of the human species can be adequately expressed. In the women's movement we demand the 'right of self-determination over our own bodies', but such an expression is inadequate to indicate that apart from the *individual* right to reproductive self-determination a large area is waiting for feminist investigation. We need to explore how being pregnant and giving birth are socially regulated. We need to find out who controls the growth of the population and its restriction. We need to know about the relationship between apparently divergent problems such as discrimination against women at work and the lack of good abortion legislation.

In the initial years of present day feminism our view of the problems of human reproduction was relatively limited. Many feminists reasoned that the invention of the contraceptive pill was a considerable step forward in the liberation of women. Women no longer had to be passive victims of sexuality. The pill meant that it would be possible, for the first time ever in history, to keep families so small that it would become easy for women to work outside the home. The right to good contraceptives and safe abortion methods was not seen as an opposition to patriarchal control over the reproductive ability of women. The battle for free abortion was seen only as a struggle with traditional ideas.

As the women's movement developed, it became clear that the relationship between women's liberation and control over pregnancy was not so clear-cut as was first supposed. It appeared that the pill may be more dangerous than good for women.[23] Moreover, the pill has been exposed as a form of contraception based on a male definition of sexual behaviour and on the constant sexual availability of women.[24] Widely available contraceptives do not mean small families. The fact that methods are available to prevent pregnancy does not necessarily mean that people make use of them. The question is: why do people want small families?

Linda Gordon began a study of the history of birth control in the United States on the assumption that contraception promised to bring an end to the only genuine handicap that women suffered – the lack of control over fertility. It is true that the technology of contraception provided women with a valuable tool, but why did the technology develop when it did?[25] We must examine under what historical circumstances the reproductive freedom of women becomes great or small and how this is connected with the development of reproductive technology.

Feminists have begun to answer these questions. Through international feminist interest about the 'body' and health care, a number of important ideas have emerged about the relationship between patriarchy, capitalism and women. A number of these are important to our discussion of 'motherhood'.

Fertilization, pregnancy, giving birth and breastfeeding seem to be outside history. They are natural functions women always had and which they will always have. But they are not natural. The only thing that is genuinely natural in these processes is that part of them that occurs within the woman's body, if it is not interfered with. The circumstances of fertilization, the knowledge women have about their own pregnancy, the fear of childbirth, the social organizations in which children are born, all vary in every culture and in every historical period. It is obvious that we should be trying to find out how different forms of biological reproduction are connected with economic and social processes within a given society, and how this is linked with the oppression of women.

Once the problem is posed it seems so obvious that we wonder why it has been left out of socialist feminist theorizing. Perhaps this is the result of the 'dual theoretical legacy' of the women's movement.[26] On the one hand there is the radical feminist analysis in which patriarchy as 'colonizer' of the woman's body occupies a central position. On the other hand there is the marxist feminist analysis in which women's oppression under capitalist conditions is central and in which emphasis is placed on the economic aspects of that oppression. The 'splitting' between body and economy reflects itself in our activities. Some women work in trade union politics and left wing parties. Others are involved in self-help, therapy and motherhood.

Socialist feminists who want to attack the problem of biological reproduction with the aid of marxist thinking risk running up against the inadequacy of traditional marxist categories and the lack of insight among left wing non-feminists that 'body' is more than 'the support of the worker and his family'.[27] They are quick to put you down as a misguided radical if you talk about historical forms of pregnancy and childbirth. The abortion battle has become a respectable arena for left wing politics, but related problems such as menstruation or pregnancy are rarely discussed. It's almost as if they think that feminism is concerned with the irrational, with keeping close to nature, with feeling without thinking. And feeling is not a historical category.

We don't have to sit squashed between an analysis of class conflicts on the one hand and an analysis of sex conflicts on the other. Over recent years various anthropological contributions have been made to the discussion on the relationship between patriarchy and capitalism. Gayle Rubin first described what she calls the 'sex-gender system': there are in every society certain systems and rules which govern how sexuality, babies and the relationships between the sexes are 'organized'.[28] Nancy Chodorow, who uses psychoanalysis to investigate how mothering is socially reproduced, analyses how the institution of motherhood is transferred from mother to daughter in this sex-gender system, what she calls the 'social organization of the sexes'.[29]

Traditional feminist thinking on biological reproduction split between two kinds of 'nature-thinking': on the one hand traditional marxist thinking, in which pregnancy and giving birth were not problematic because they are natural, and on the other hand traditional radical feminist thinking, in which pregnancy and childbirth are a natural handicap for women. Thinking in terms of a social system in which relationships between women and men are regulated is a great step forward.

Various studies have revealed that the ability of women to control their own bodies was not always as restricted as it is now. A small but important discovery for the women's movement was that there has always been birth control in some form or another. In ancient Egypt, women used pessaries and there was considerable knowledge of spermicides. Accounts of this are amusing and inspiring.[30] What must be explained, therefore, is not the origin of birth control but its prohibition and its suppression (in the Netherlands prohibition came in the twentieth century through public morality legislation).[31]

Another important discovery for feminists was that the present sexist system of medical care with its modern childbirth technology flourishes at the expense of women's control over their own bodies. Well known studies in this field by Barbara Ehrenreich, by Deirdre English, and by Ann Oakley expose the active expulsion of women from medical professions and the demotion of the work of midwives.[32] The Netherlands is one of the few Western countries where medical intervention in childbirth has not yet assumed the horrifying proportions of the United States. But in the Netherlands too there are developments in this direction. The number of artificially induced births is increasing and more and more women are connected up to an apparatus which monitors the whole birth process,[33] even when this is not medically necessary.

It is ironic that feminist opposition to the 'theft of childbirth' immediately evokes two reactions. One is the reproach from the left that it is not 'political' to be involved in the relationships in which people become pregnant and have children. The other is the reproach from feminists who want to return to prehistory, leapfrog over the intricacies of technology back into the Stone Age to suffer pain.[34] Feminist opposition to the medical model of childbirth should not be interpreted as an opposition to technology itself but as an opposition to the social organization of technology, to the patriarchy of medicine, to man's control over woman.

A third discovery, or rather one which overlaps the two former ones, is that a relationship exists between capitalism, imperialism, population policies and women. History demonstrates how the motherhood of women is manipulated to increase or decrease the birth rate.[35] Again and again we hear how, under the pressure of imperialist interests, attempts are made to deliberately restrict population growth in Third World countries, how the fertility of women is controlled as a means to counter mounting social unrest.[36]

All these insights have made clear how crucial the control over our bodies is for the liberation of women. In recent years we have witnessed an important development of the movement – for women's repossesion of their bodies will bring far more essential changes to human society than will the workers' seizure of the means of production.[37]

2. Domestic and public

Marijke Mossink

Introduction

Throughout history and in most contemporary societies, women's
access to public life has been circumscribed by conditions. At the
end of the last century Brussels etiquette dictated that genteel ladies
could go no further than twelve houses from their own home
unless chaperoned.[1] The first Dutch feminists incurred general
scorn by making speeches in public.[2] Aletta Jacobs remembers
how she wanted to ignore the custom that hindered her from
walking down the Kalverstraat (main road) at certain times of day
and going to the theatre on her own. She writes that a policeman
admonished her with the words, 'Just stay at home in the evenings,
then you won't run into trouble on the street', when she
complained to him about a man who tried to sexually assault her –
something many women have experienced.[3] In Islamic countries
women may only go out if they are wearing a veil. The Islamic
revolution meant the return of the chador, a shawl that covers
head and body. You don't see groups of women hanging around
on the terraces in Mediterranean countries all day. Among the
Mundurucú Indians in South America women may only go
outside the village in groups. Any woman who goes out alone is
outlawed and punished by multiple rape.[4]

These examples show how space is divided between women and
men. This is related to the sexual division of labour and our
sexuality. Women are forbidden to go where it is considered they
have no social function. Women should not be sitting in cafes.
They should be at home doing the housework. A hundred years
ago a respectable woman did her embroidery, stayed at home, and

certainly did not go strolling along the Kalverstraat (main road) or make speeches.

> Man for the field and woman for the hearth;
> Man for the sword and for the needle she;
> Man with the head and woman with the heart;
> Man to command and woman to obey;
> All else confusion.[5]

The American marxist Eli Zaretsky put the above poem on the cover of his book about the capitalist division between the waged work of men and the domestic work of women.[6] Domestic sphere and public sphere are the concepts we use to indicate that a division exists between the world of women and the world of men. This essay is about those concepts. They are used in the women's movement to indicate not only the spatial division between the sexes, but also to describe women's oppression as a whole. The world of men, politics, state, law, police, army, science, culture, is regarded as the world of power. Women have no access to it. Feminist activities have long been opposed to this division between domestic and public spheres. In suffrage campaigns and in the struggle for the right to education and work the nineteenth century feminist movement demanded access to the public sphere for women.

Our organization Dolle Mina, wanted public toilets for women, access to the diplomatic academy of Nijenrode and crèches to give women the opportunity to be more than household drudges.[7] Every year we demonstrate for our right to walk the streets. Recently we have made demands which would allow men to spend more time at home and do more in the domestic sphere, namely, a five-hour working day for everyone, and paternity leave for men.

The division between domestic and public spheres has not only been identified by feminists. In studies about women in capitalist development, the origin or existence of a division between the women's world and men's world is recognized by many authors. It appears in studies on middle-class women in Victorian England, women in eighteenth and nineteenth century America, housewives, and the first women's movement.[8] In Zaretsky's book the division between domestic and public is central. For him the existence of the division is almost synonymous with women's oppression. Domestic and public can be applied not only to the western women's oppression; feminist anthropologists have revealed how women in other cultures are also associated with the domestic sphere.

Concepts are not neutral or value free. They have both a scientific and a political meaning. The terms domestic sphere and public sphere are not a feminist invention. They take on a feminist meaning when feminists use them to understand women's oppression. This article tackles two questions: what knowledge of women is gained by using the terms domestic and public and what is the political significance of these terms for women's studies, in particular for feminist anthropology?[9] I have tried to answer these questions by tracing my own history using the terms. This essay is, therefore, my own story,[10] – my struggle and my doubts. At the end I draw a number of general conclusions.

In the first part of the essay I look into how these terms are used by feminist anthropologists. They were initially concepts that made sense of women's oppression in a scientific way. I also discuss four articles that have been important for me. They comprise an analysis of women's power in Mediterranean cultures within the theoretical framework of domestic sphere/public sphere. Then I elaborate my criticisms of the use of the domestic/public framework as a general theoretical framework for the analysis of women's oppression. Lastly I make a number of suggestions for study in which the terms domestic sphere and public sphere could be useful.

Five or six years ago I was planning some research into the political relations in a small town in southern Italy. My stay there confronted me once again with the division between women's world and men's world. This division also exists in the Netherlands but in southern Italy I saw that women were literally imprisoned in the home and family. So I became interested in the anthropology of the Mediterranean as well as feminist anthropology. There was not yet much information available. A group was formed in 1975 at the anthropological institute of Leyden University which began to investigate women and development.[11] I also knew of the

Vrouwengroep Antropologie (Women and Anthropology Group), a student seminar group at Amsterdam University.[12] Apart from this, there was a sparse literature, a few articles, some monographs and a few collections of essays. In one of them, *Women, Culture and Society*,[13] I found many of the questions I was facing: what does the division between women and men mean? How did it originate? How does the division affect women's work? How does it affect women's social standing, influence and power? Is women's sphere really as unimportant as suggested in anthropological literature? Is what men do more important? How has this come about? Why are women kept locked into the world of children, household and family?

The American anthropologist Michelle Rosaldo was the first person I came across who tried to deal systematically with these questions. In her article, 'Woman, Culture and Society: a Theoretical Overview',[14] she develops an analysis based on the domestic sphere and the public sphere. She argues that anthropology is an academic discipline in which 'femininity' and 'masculinity' are concepts whose meaning alters according to the society being studied. She believes however that the asymmetry between the sexes is universal and that this asymmetry can be traced to an opposition between 'domestic' and 'public'.[15] Women are always associated with the 'domestic': the social sphere of bringing up children and kinship-relations, a cultural consequence of their biological ability to bear children. Men are always oriented to the 'public', the outside world, the sphere of authority and superiority. This division is so universal that Michelle Rosaldo concludes that 'the opposition between domestic and public orientations (an opposition that must, in part, derive from the nurturant capacities of women) provides the necessary framework for an examination of male and female roles in any society'.[16] According to her, this framework provides a basis for the study of any aspect of the inequality between the sexes including personality and its formation, formal male power versus informal female power, the association of women with 'nature' and men with 'culture', man as norm and woman as deviation, women's work and men's work.[17]

Michelle Rosaldo's argument is convincing. The opposition between domestic and public spheres can be observed in all areas where there is inequality between women and men. You don't have to be a feminist to see that men dominate women, or to relate the differences between women and men to the sexual division of tasks between them. Nor is it necessarily feminist to notice that a universal division exists between the world of women (the domestic sphere) and that of men (the public sphere). It is not difficult to notice the division. The association between women and the domestic sphere and men and the public sphere occurs in the work of many academics and anthropologists who are apologists for patriarchy.

Domestic sphere and public sphere only became feminist concepts when it became clear to feminists that for traditional academics the association of women with the domestic sphere results from chains of association which begin with female 'nature'. Feminist researchers refused to accept this. For them domestic sphere and public sphere were the starting point for a search to uncover the chain of association and to place a question mark at each link: womb – giving birth – suckling – nurturing – household – family – domestic sphere and womb – earthly – close to nature – conservative – vulnerable – needing protection – apolitical – domestic sphere and womb – mammal – maternal – loving – emotional – irrational – concrete – not capable of abstract thought – closer to nature than culture – domestic sphere.

The search began less than fifteen years ago and has not been easy. Decades earlier Margaret Mead cut through some important links in the chain of associations with her intercultural comparison of 'femininity' and 'masculinity'. But the generation studying at the end of the 1960s had to begin again to supply proof that women's oppression is not a 'natural' phenomenon.[18] In academic culture the chain of associations between female 'nature' and women's place in the domestic sphere lay submerged in a thick muddy layer of contempt, disinterest and neglect. 'Traditional' anthropologists concerned with kinship structures – domestic sphere! – could not ignore women, but the association of women with bringing up children and nurturing was so self-evident, that they rarely bothered to look deeper at the causes and implications behind it. The example of Robin Fox illustrates this well.

The English anthropologist, Robin Fox, wrote a standard work on kinship and marriage which has been obligatory reading for generations of students.[19] According to Robin Fox any kinship structure, i.e. the social organization of blood relationship and relationship by marriage, is based on four fixed principles.[20] The first and second are that women bear children and that men impregnate women. The third is that men generally exercise control. The fourth principle is that close relatives do not have sexual relations with one another. Fox states that the first and second principles are irrefutable but have social implications. These are extensively examined later in the book. The same goes for the fourth principle, the prohibition on incest. Fox acknowledges that it is possible to doubt the third principle, male power. But he, however, finds objections 'somehow unreal'. According to Fox, men exercise control in the majority of all known kinship structures and 'for very good reasons'. The 'sheer physiological facts of existence' make women's contribution to decision making processes secondary to that of the man at any level higher than the 'purely domestic' (Fox, p. 32). Fox argues that women are busy with their 'highly specialized task' of bearing and bringing up children, so the men must go hunting, fight enemies and make the decisions. That brief explanation is all there is to justify the third principle. The argument does not even merit its own chapter, as the fourth principle – the prohibition on incest – does.[21]

This is an example of the anthropology in which male domination of women and the association of women with domestic work are explained by biology.[22] I did not come to anthropology through the traditional study of 'primitive tribes' and kinship structures. I studied political science and took up anthropology because of my interest in the political economy of other cultures. But in materialist and marxist anthropology as well as traditional anthropology women are associated with the domestic sphere, albeit in a less explicit manner. The 'left' anthropology that formed my introduction to the subject was totally focused on the public sphere, barely noticing the domestic sphere and its social relations.[23] The concern was with capitalism and imperialism in the Third World, with property relations and power relations, with class structures and peasant revolutions. What was always presupposed but never stated was that this is all a male concern.

Sexist academics, of whatever persuasion, view the division between domestic and public as an inevitable result of the division of labour between the sexes, a division of labour which is based on biological realities. Women are reduced to nature and thus disappear as subjects for social scientists. Feminist anthropologists would not accept this division and its implications for women. 'Domestic' and 'public' were also precisely the terms which caused me to doubt that women's oppression is 'natural'. To me, it seemed that 'domestic' and public' were the first attempts to develop scientific sociological concepts in order to develop a theory of women's oppression.[24]

'Domestic and public', when used by feminists, make women into active subjects within their own reality. As feminists we refuse to accept that women do not organize within their world of children and home. The domestic and public framework made it possible to investigate the unacknowledged exercise of power by women in the domestic sphere, and their attempts to influence the outside world as well as their political and economic contribution to society.

This investigation was not only of academic importance. The popularity of the domestic and public framework among feminist academics also relates to its political importance. We demanded not only that scientific attention be paid to the absence of women in the sphere of public power, we also demanded political attention. We wanted recognition of the importance of women's work in the sphere where they predominate. This is an academic as well as a political demand. The division between domestic and public seemed universal. From the political viewpoint that gave us a bond with women elsewhere, our exclusion from the public sphere corresponded with theirs. Our political refusal to tolerate a situation which had nothing to do with biology but everything to do with male power, complemented our academic search for places where women have power and where their position is less marginal. The very idea of women's power was inspiring.

We were searching, therefore, for women, their work, their influence and positions of power, and the ideologies which assume and confirm their 'inferiority'. We had questions and enthusiasm, but few answers. The investigations of feminist anthropologists fanned out over a number of fields.[25] I went in search of a framework to study Italian women in poor southern rural societies. I found a number of articles which examined the position of women in other Mediterranean countries using the domestic and public framework. Initially, I thought it was what I was looking for. But gradually my questions changed and the answers I found in my reading of the literature no longer sufficed. Eventually I found the analysis presented in these articles inadequate and the conclusions mistaken. I began to wonder whether the domestic and public framework obscured more than it clarified. The following section outlines growing doubts.

Friedl, Riegelhaupt, Nelson and Rogers: four well known American anthropologists, whose articles I know by heart.[26] All four have carried out research on women in the Mediterranean area, investigating women's influence and their power. In contrast to most anthropologists who never acknowledge women's influence at all, or who regard their position as totally marginal, these writers acknowledge women's influence and women's power. No wonder the articles became important to me. I discovered them at a time when I was just beginning to ask questions about women. The articles afforded me good insights. There were also points that did not satisfy me. It was the points I was critical of that eventually led me to the idea that the domestic and public framework might be unsuitable for a serious analysis of the causes of women's oppression.

Ernestine Friedl wrote about a Greek village, Vasilika,[27] where there was a sharp division between women and men. The public, political sphere in the village was exclusively reserved for men. Work on the small farmsteads was divided according to sex. Women did all the work in the house (looking after children and housework) and men did practically all the work on the land. Jobs around and close to the house were shared.

The men in Vasilika enjoyed higher prestige than the women in every way. But, said Friedl, the appearance of male power is deceptive. In the domestic sphere of the family women had authority. They had sources of power. One of them, Friedl suggests, was the possession of land: women often brought land that they had inherited into the marriage. Women also had an important 'negative power', as Friedl calls it: 'their willingness to behave chastely, modestly and becomingly, which is a prime necessity for the maintenance of the feeling of men's self-esteem.'[28] Women did not behave like this without making men aware of it, they complained often and loudly and did not let men forget how important their contribution was.

Ernestine Friedl's conclusion is that if you accept that the domestic sphere forms the most important social unit of a society, then you must direct your attention towards it and not to the less important public sphere. In Vasilika the family was the most important social unit; the division of power between sexes in the family was more important than that in public life. In the family the power of women and the power of men were complementary to one another. Both sexes shared decision-making. Appearances deceive. Public male prestige does not correspond with reality. Women are not powerless. Ernestine Friedl is concerned mainly with power relationships within the family. She doesn't say what her conclusion about the power of women in the family means for the division of power in Vasilika, or for Greek society.

Another American anthropologist, Joyce Riegelhaupt, goes further. She was a research worker in Portugal, in a village near Lisbon, during Salazar's regime. At that time women formally and politically had no rights at all. But, says Riegelhaupt, you must look further than public legal and political structures. The women in 'her village' had a far-reaching political influence. They had more contacts than men, both inside and outside the village and they knew how to use them to obtain improvements in the village. The women acquired these contacts in two ways. Women saw each other throughout the day in the village, while men worked outside the village on the land. Most women also had contacts with 'higher-placed persons' in Lisbon, because most of them had been maids there before marriage. The women therefore had an advantage over men when it came to obtaining information and using it. Just like in Vasilika, the women in the Portuguese village showed that male power is deceptive.

The anthropologist Cynthia Nelson also holds that significant female power can be found in the domestic sphere. She looked at ethnographic literature on societies in the Middle East where the division between women and men was more extreme than in Greece or Portugal. According to Nelson the total segregation of women is superficial and conceals the reality of women's influence. Women occupy crucial positions in family relationships even if only between their husband's family and their own. They pass information in both directions, or withhold it. So, they influence the decisions men take. Women form groups together and that is a source of strength. They support one another and exercise an important social control. Nelson finds it worthwhile to regard the domestic sphere not as the place where women are shut up because they have no access to the public sphere, but as the place where women have mutual contacts to the exclusion of men.

There is an important source of power for women in the Middle East: women's relation to the supernatural. 'Through witchcraft, sorcery, divination and curing, women are instrumental in influencing the lives of men.'[29] Cynthia Nelson concludes that it is a mistake to regard the domestic sphere and the public sphere as completely separate. The two spheres touch at so many points that they can only be understood in relation to each other. In Nelson's view women 'negotiate' with men in the public sphere from their position in the domestic sphere. They have significant power and can apply sanctions and exercise control.

All three authors strongly emphasize how important the domestic sphere is if society is to function. They indicate how women's influence is substantial, an influence which can't be seen if you only pay attention to the formal power of the public sphere. The three articles suggest that a structure of informal women's power, complementary to formal male power, can be distinguished by any careful observer. This is an important insight.

The last writer I want to discuss, Susan Carol Rogers, did research in north-eastern France.[30] She carries the reasoning through to the point of standing relationships on their heads. Her opinion is that in traditional agrarian societies the public sphere is not important and the power of men has no foundation. In those societies only the domestic sphere is important and, according to Rogers, the women have authority. To explain the appearance of male power, Rogers suggests that a mutual dependence exists between women and men which guarantees that men are under the impression that they are the masters, whereas the women are satisfied with making all the important decisions from behind a façade of powerlessness. Susan Carol Rogers elaborates this to a model which she claims explains all the contradictions in the relations between women and men, and which explains what happens if circumstances alter when modernization of agriculture occurs or when peasants become wage-workers. Then male power may become genuine.

In retrospect I think that all four of these articles were important as a counterbalance to the sexist anthropologists who did not see women as important and who found the domestic sphere un-interesting. It was important for me because it showed that women try to control reality, something which affects families and also the public sphere of economic and political decisions.[31]

It is a pity, however, that the writers of these articles systemati-cally distort the reality of male dominance, something which bears little resemblance to the myth Susan Rogers makes of it. The importance of the public sphere is underestimated by Friedl and altogether by Rogers. Both are of the opinion that in 'traditional societies' marginal to the modern industrial world the public sphere of village politics is not powerful and power therefore lies with whoever makes the decisions in the domestic sphere. I find such an analysis inaccurate. It is true that the peasants they write about hardly have any say about their own living conditions. They cannot control land-lease conditions, access to markets, distribu-tion of property or class relations. But if men lack power that doesn't mean that women possess it. You can only share Friedl's and Rogers's conclusion that women have just as much – or more – power as men if you ignore that men as a *class* have little to say, but as a *gender* they have a substantial share in the power structures of patriarchy. Public political and economic practices are on their side. The culture which gives them authority perpetuates their superiority. Family legislation also gives them power to oppress women. It should be obvious that we should look at whether and how, these powerless farmers make up for their lack of power as a class with their power as part of the male sex.

In the articles by Nelson and Riegelhaupt women's influence in the public sphere is overrated. Women try to get their own way and try to influence the decisions of men, by giving or not giving information, or by doing so precisely at the right moment. But you only have to look at the instruments of power that women use to realize that you can distinguish between sly, informal female power and public, legitimate male power. Gossip, whispers, chatter, witchcraft, manipulation and bustle are all signs of powerlessness. 'Rattling one's chains' Anja Meulenbelt calls this 'power' of women.[32] Women are 'fish always swimming upstream', according to Dolores in Marilyn French's novel *The Bleeding Heart*.[33] The anthropologist Susan Harding characterizes the power of women in poor agrarian societies: '*If* women have any power to affect the conditions of their lives it is through men and on an individual basis. This is the hallmark of the subordinate position in a hierarchical relationship: the prohibition, whether implicit or explicit, of deliberate collective action to effect a change in living conditions.'[34] She points out that the power of women does not have any cumulative effect. Every gain is temporary. The battle is constantly being fought.[35] Recognized authority is not maintained this way.

The articles also overlook the power of men in the domestic sphere. The writers have not looked for it. It is not true that women pull all the strings. The power of men extends to relationships in the home. Ultimately men rule sexuality, reproduction and motherhood.

All four articles are characterized by the writers' enthusiasm. They are so intent on demonstrating that women are important, that they see female power in what I would rather regard as powerlessness. They deny the power of men where it is present. In two cases there is an explanation. Friedl and Riegelhaupt published their articles at a time (1967) when a feminist anthropology hardly existed. Then the most important concern was to convince established academics that women are interesting and that the world would collapse without their work and without the domestic sphere. The work of Rogers and Nelson is later (1975) but they still concentrate on how important women are. When Nelson turns against the view that there is a total division between the domestic sphere and the public sphere in the Middle East, it is directed against the sexist view, which ascribes no political importance whatsoever to the domestic sphere. In Rogers's case, it is not clear why in 1975 she concludes that male power in 'traditional peasant societies' is a myth. Perhaps because her view of those societies is rather idealist, she makes caricatures of the rustic life. She leaves aside imperialism, capitalist exploitation and oppression and looks only at relationships within the village.

It can be said that all four articles are written to challenge sexist anthropology. They question the assumption that the domestic sphere is uninteresting and that nothing happens there that is politically important. In that sense they cut through one of the links in the chain of associations about women. They make it clear that the domestic sphere is a political sphere, just as much as the public sphere.

There it stops. The rest of the chain remains intact. The writers of all four articles identify a division between women and men and look at the consequences for power relations between women and men. They start with the assumption that the division between domestic sphere and public sphere is based on the division of labour between the sexes, but they accept that division of labour. They do not look for its precise meaning for women, nor for its origins. To them it is self evident that women have children, are mothers, look after house and hearth. Sexuality is not discussed. They don't tell us where the domestic and public division comes from or why the division exists. The articles situate the power relations between women and men in the division itself and that comes close to thinking that the inequality between women and men exists because a division exists between domestic and public sphere.

That leads me to question whether the terms domestic sphere and public sphere are more confusing than clarifying, if you don't keep firmly in mind that they are at the end of a long series of power relations and that they therefore are a consequence, an effect, rather than a cause.[36] Domestic and public are used as 'container' concepts. Everything can be put into them and all the oppositions between women and men can be accommodated by them. You also see this in Michelle Rosaldo's work.[37] The terms domestic sphere and public sphere are also loosely used as synonyms for reproduction and production. Everything women do is 'reproduction' and all reproduction is 'domestic', everything men do is 'production' and all production is 'public'. That is not adequate as other investigators have noted.[38]

Domestic/public is a theoretical framework with division as its centre. But that division is the result of power relationships which preceded it. The point is that we should look for connections instead of divisions and for those relations in which the power of men over women is established. The domestic and public framework appears all-embracing, but in fact it reduces the relation between the sexes to one dimension. That is much too simple. Patriarchal power has many dimensions and is produced in many relationships; in labour and labour power, in sexuality, motherhood, children and ideology. We need concepts for all these relationships in order to describe, to comprehend, to explain, to specify and to relate.

It is difficult to develop good, unambiguous concepts as is seen from the attempts to develop a marxist feminist conceptual framework for analyzing women's oppression. At the moment these attempts appear to have yielded little more than a labyrinth of production and reproduction: the reproduction of production and the reproduction of reproduction. More self-control is required in introducing new terms and less reverence should be accorded to the marxist tradition of saying difficult things in a difficult way. More importantly the 'production and reproduction debate' is based on an insight that patriarchal power is a complex phenomenon while the domestic and public framework suggests that it isn't so bad.

There is another important reason to seek concepts for the analysis of women's oppression which are based on a connection. We lack a dynamic, historical element because the domestic and public framework lacks it. A relationship has two partners. You can look at relationships from two sides and detect resistance and conflict from both.

This does not mean that I am in favour of eradicating the concepts domestic sphere and public sphere from the arsenal of concepts for studying women's oppression. An apparently universal division exists between the world of women and men. That division is important in the way relations between the genders are regulated in various societies. I am in favour of indicating the power relations which result in the division between the world of women and of men. We should use concepts which have been developed for those relationships and not to just accommodate them in the domestic/public definition. The terms domestic sphere and public sphere can be reserved for describing and analyzing the phenomenon to which they primarily refer: the geographical distribution of space between women and men, together with the division of labour that exists between them.

So I return to the observation with which I began. Women are denied access to or admitted to certain positions only under certain conditions. If the concepts domestic sphere and public sphere are used only to analyze that phenomenon they can contribute to our knowledge of specific forms of women's oppression. The central question then becomes: how does the control mechanism of male power rely on men's control of access to space?

We should now proceed to examine the division between domestic sphere and public sphere in such a way as to specify instead of lumping everything together. There are countless questions and possibilities for research.

We could begin by examining whether there is a clear border between the 'women's world' and the 'men's world' and where precisely that border is. In our own society it is not a clear line. In the town in southern Italy where I worked, you could have drawn the borderline with a piece of chalk. There were two public squares, one intended for men, the other for women, their children and their families. The border is 'guarded', there are penalties for overstepping it. The prospect of multiple rape among the Mundurucú Indians is an extreme example. But 'penalties' do not have to be so dramatic. The usual penalty for entering the male world of the street is whistling, breast-pinching, bottom-pinching and 'jokes' about your legs.

Women can enter the public sphere unpunished if accompanied by a spouse, a chaperone, or a group of women. A good alibi also serves: shopping or enjoying art and culture. We could also examine the ideologies which justify the existence of a division between women's world and men's world. These exist blatantly in the media, science, Sunday sermons and also in an internalized way in the individual psyche. More women than men suffer from agoraphobia, and therapists state that husbands of agoraphobic patients generally oppose therapy.[39]

A series of questions can be asked to find out whether a specific border, a specific prohibition is valid for all women, or for special categories of women with the same civil status, age or class. In the first anthropological village study of Sicily, some fifty years ago, it is recorded that married women could move about more freely than unmarried girls and very old women could easily go out in the street on their own. This was not true for upper class women in the village. They never left the house unless accompanied. Women in families of rich peasants and craftsmen imitated this – even a small child counted as a chaperone.[40] Sicily has changed, but even in the 1970s women's freedom of movement is still limited. A teacher from Enna tells that her father only lets her go dancing if her brother is there to keep watch over her: 'The boy I dance with is not allowed to say anything at all, for if he [the brother] sees him open his mouth, he comes between us. "Put your coat on, we're going home [. . .]" Of course the result has been that I prefer to stay home.'[41]

It is not always clear where the 'border' runs between domestic and public, women's and men's world. Therefore it is to be expected that women get confused about what is allowed and what is not. There are more questions too. Are women confronted with conflicting demands? Where do these demands come from? How do women resolve them? The English anthropologist Renée Hirschon describes how women in Piraeus, near Athens, must stay at home particularly just after their wedding day and just after the birth of a child. It is thought that at those times they are even more vulnerable than usual to the dangers that face women on the street. But then there is not always someone available to do the shopping. The solution is '. . . mothers of newborn babies do have to go to the local shop sometimes, but they should always avoid going into the shop and should stay outside on the threshhold'.[42]

You can look at the domestic sphere in the way Cynthia Nelson suggested, as a place from which under certain conditions, men are excluded.[43] In some societies the women's bathhouse is an important place for social contact between women. In America it is the 'little girls' room', the rest room where women can withdraw together to plan the evening out with their boyfriends . . . Our own women's houses are examples of a women's sanctuary which is safe from men and there the revolution is forged.

That brings me to more questions for feminist research. Do women fight against their confinement to a women's world? How do they do it? Do women want the right to cross the border or do they want to abolish the border? Do women fight for the expansion of their own domain, or for its abolition? It is intriguing to ask questions about change. What is the history of the division between domestic and public? Has the 'border' shifted, or has it stayed in the same place? We can often do what our grandmothers couldn't do. The opposite also occurs. Increasing prosperity often means decreased freedom of movement for women. A man who 'no longer has to let his wife work' can shut her up at home.

The terms domestic sphere and public sphere can be placed in a broader analytic framework. Control of space, access to space, is an important instrument of power. Women must 'know their place'. But with the aid of the question that I have asked we can investigate how this is instilled into them. We can find out how men maintain their power over women's freedom of movement and also how women sometimes successfully oppose this.

An important question remains. Why is control over women's freedom of movement so important and why are women often so horribly punished when they break the rules? The question cannot be answered by using the concepts domestic sphere and public sphere. Other concepts are necessary, concepts that refer to the relationships in which the men's power over labour, sexuality, motherhood, the mind and the feelings of women is acknowledged. These relationships ultimately determine whether or not women can gather roots and fruits outside the village and whether or not they run the danger of a slap in the face if they go for a stroll late in the evening.

3. The dual heritage

Joyce Outshoorn

> We are pulled in one direction by a marxist feminist analysis of the socio-economic bases of women's oppression, and in another direction by a radical feminist focus on male control of women's bodies as the key to patriarchy. Our differences have not hampered the ad hoc coalitions formed around struggles for abortion and protection against sterilization abuse; for affirmative action, maternity leave and day care, for the Equal Rights Amendment and the right of sexual preference. But differences in theoretical position do affect our broader social commitments and political alliances. They affect our conception of the scope of the women's movement; its relation to issues of race and class; and specifically, whether or how to join with what are still male-dominant movements of resistance to inequities stemming from an imperialist organization of the world economy and society.[1]

This quotation from an article by the American feminist historian Joan Kelly summarizes a tension which is familiar to most activists in the women's movement: the tension between job and housework, party politics and trade unions, sex roles and one's body, motherhood and social life. We also see this tension in our activities between 'political activists' who work in 'hard male politics' and women who work in consciousness-raising groups and projects directed against sexual violence or violence against women; between the 'hard' and the 'soft'. We also encounter this tension in discussions about alliances: whether or not to form a separate women's group; whether or not to become involved in a 'men's' party; whether or not to turn our attention to racism, the environment, nuclear energy. In the theory too, there is a duality, in spite of the growth of socialist feminist theory. On one hand there are traditional marxist theories which talk about the reserve army of labour, female unemployment and analyze how cuts and the economic crisis affect women, while motherhood is reduced to mere reproduction of the labour force. On the other hand we have new radical feminist analyses of sexual violence as misogyny, and profound explorations of motherhood, while complex economic relations are lumped together under the heading of 'capitalism' or simply 'society'.

Most socialist feminists will agree that both views are relevant for an analysis of women's oppression. We continually use parts of both traditions. Some say capitalism and patriarchy, others patriarchy and capitalism (emphasizing one or other according to their political preference. But the crucial question remains: what is the relationship between them and how are they interwoven?

Lines from the past

Viewed historically, the tension in theory and politics is not only a dilemma of the contemporary women's movement. Precursors of the nineteenth century women's movement, such as Mary Woll-stonecraft, Elizabeth Cady Stanton and Harriet Taylor Mill,[2] already had a clear insight into the power men have over women and into the disastrous effects of a strict division of labour between women and men. But they did not see that this was rooted in capitalism. They argued that women should have equal rights and equal opportunities on the basis that they are just as rational as men. This gave them optimistic expectations of women's entry into 'male fields' such as politics and the professions. Today these women can be described as progressive liberals.

The socialist women's movement refers back to the patriarchs Marx and Engels and their views on women's oppression.[3] Friedrich Engels certainly knew where to look for a comprehensive theory on women's oppression. In the introduction to his well-known *The Origin of the Family, Private Property and the State*[4] he identifies production and reproduction as decisive moments in history, and so acknowledges the importance of the reproduction of the human race and the relations within. But since Engels the marxist tradition has only emphasized the relations within production, so no satisfactory theory about women's oppression has emerged. For that reason too there has been no comprehensive marxist theory of society and its development, for this cannot be developed unless the relations between women and men and the reproduction of the human race are included.

The political ideas flowing from these orthodox analyses are easily summarized. Anyone like me, who has a left wing past, will be familiar with it: women are oppressed by capitalism, their salvation lies in paid work outside the home, then they can wage the class war for socialism, together with men. Only then will women be truly liberated. This is a denial of precapitalist patriarchal relations and also of independent women's struggle. Over the years we have become, however, adept at refuting this stale orthodoxy.

Another consequence of the theory has received less attention from feminists, but to me seems just as important. If the relations within which reproduction of the human race occur are not questioned it is easy to presume they are natural. The strength of marxist theory lies in its explanation that social phenomena have developed historically, and are not immutable. If we assume that the relations of reproduction are fixed, on the other hand, we are then forced to accept that biology determines women's destiny . . . illogical but something both men of the left and men of the right generally agree about. Women are beginning to understand that reproduction is ruled by patriarchal relations too and that men define and control how biology determines female sexuality.

From the very beginning of the modern women's movement feminists have paid attention to this area. Kate Millett, in *Sexual Politics*,[5] was the first to introduce the word 'patriarchy' into the women's movement in order to distinguish between sexual domination and class domination. She made it clear that science, religion and myth, the body and sexuality are all affected by patriarchy. Shulamith Firestone in *The Dialectic of Sex*[6] said women's oppression springs from the fact that women bear and bring up the children. She pointed to the power of the ideal of romantic love and identified what she called 'men's inability to love'. She also pointed out the oppression of children. The emphasis on 'patriarchy' became the foundation of radical feminism, and as a result, subsequent writing has concentrated on themes such as the body, sexuality and sexual violence. Juliet Mitchell, although clearly distancing herself from radical feminism, in *Women's Estate*[7] also emphasized the distinction between biological reproduction and sexuality.

Domestic labour

Although Juliet Mitchell criticized radical feminism, she was also dissatisfied with classical marxist theory. She wanted to retain marxist methods of analysis, but said 'we should ask the feminist questions, but try to come up with some marxist answers.'[8] She found class relations and the capitalist mode of production central to explanation of women's oppression. Early attempts to synthesize socialist and feminist views were based on capitalism as a starting point, and the main question for many women in the movement became how women's oppression is institutionalized by capitalism. This led to historical research and to asking what was specifically capitalist in women's oppression. It emerged that the role of housewife as a female ideal was only a recent historical development. So radical feminists (and Engels) were right and other marxists were wrong. And as patriarchy existed before capitalism, capitalism was no longer the only enemy. Socialist feminists then had two dragons to slay: both capitalism and patriarchy.

The main theme of the early discussion about the connection between socialism and feminism became the debate about the nature of domestic labour. This was carried on both in England and in the Netherlands.[9] In the course of this debate, the argument became centred on the relationship between domestic labour, capitalism and its relations of production. The importance of domestic labour for the reproduction of labour power was also examined. A number of analyses about the shortcomings of this debate have appeared. Maureen Mackintosh points out that the debate ignores the fact that domestic labour is carried out under certain social relations, in which men dominate women, and the women do the domestic work.[10] Nothing new on this emerged from the debate, which is why, Mackintosh thinks, the English women's movement quickly lost interest in it. (Another reason is doubtless that it led yet again to obscure academic marxist theorizing.) Maxine Molyneux remarks that the debate lost its feminist character because participants never questioned why women not men do domestic work.[11] Neither was it made clear how domestic work as socially necessary labour influences women's oppression. The attention given to washing up, vacuuming and looking after a husband diverted attention from the problem of childcare.[12] Jean Gardiner, one of the participants in the debate, remarked in a lecture delivered at the Free University of Amsterdam that the debate placed emphasis on how the capitalist class profits from the work of housewives rather than on how men profit.[13] The idea that housewives work for love, disappeared; the ideology of romantic love had already been exposed – through CR groups but also through Firestone's excellent piece in *The Dialectic of Sex* ('Chapter 6 may change your life!' is written on the book jacket).

The debate on domestic labour nevertheless took steps towards developing a theory of women's oppression. It clarified what was common to women of all classes and how housewives make an essential contribution to society. It demonstrated that women's oppression will not be removed by mere 'education', 'information', 'change of mentality' or 'role-breaking' alone. Women's oppression is an integral part of capitalist relations and without structural changes it will continue. Put another way: women's oppression is not part of the 'super-structure', but has a 'material base'. The debate can be traced in the minutes and discussion documents of numerous political groups, in the references to 'inside and outside the home', or in the recognition that domestic labour is socially necessary.

The analysis of biological reproduction

The debate on domestic labour placed the emphasis on the relations of production and on the economic significance of domestic labour. Motherhood, childbirth and childcare were put into the same category as housework. This was a step backwards compared with Juliet Mitchell's analysis. Mitchell demonstrated that four functions came together in the modern nuclear family: the reproduction of children, the regulation of sexuality, socialization and domestic labour. Although she couldn't sort out whether reproduction is merely reproduction of the species or also reproduction of the labour force[14] she did distinguish housework and reproduction as separate problems, each demanding its own solution. This is the basis for her opposition to crude slogans such as 'abolish the family'. In her view, such a slogan fails to demonstrate any insight into the processes in the family and hence offers no solutions.[15] The views of Firestone and Millett have also temporarily faded into the background.

The above writers all offered useful starting points for a discussion about the problems of biological reproduction, yet the early women's movement in the Netherlands only looked at the subject indirectly. Motherhood and childbirth were viewed with suspicion and distrust, because they were traditionally seen as the way women should fulfil themselves. The result was that more attention was given to *not* being a mother (abortion, contraception) and to reducing the 'inconveniences' of motherhood (crèches, adjusted school hours, part time work) than to investigating how motherhood could be non-oppressive.[16] We still had no coherent theory of 'body-politics'. At most we made the basic demand for the right to control our own bodies.

If my terminology about reproduction, sexuality and motherhood is vague and I refer instead to 'body-politics', this is an indication of our lack of theory. There is still no theory which has the depth or the range of the theory about capitalism. So little has been developed that it is possible for 'left-wingers' to completely dismiss 'body-politics'. Two objections to the theories of Millett and Firestone hindered the development of a 'body-theory'. They both viewed patriarchy as eternal, monolithic and unalterable, and Firestone herself made biology absolute, saying it was the reason for women's oppression. The objections to the theory made by socialist feminists, were almost too effective and almost the entire 'body' analysis was dismissed, leaving the field to the debate on domestic labour. Discussions about the body then developed in other sections of the women's movement, reinforced by the work of feminists whose historical or anthropological work eventually revived the debate. Through a combination of practical and political work, it became clear that biology need not be women's destiny and the women's movement developed new policy about control of the 'body' in campaigns about violence against women, rape, health care and pornography, in addition to abortion and birth control.

But the duality remained and it was difficult to make a theoretical connection between radical feminist views and marxist analyses. The marxist theories were essentially unchanged despite some genuflecting in the direction of domestic labour, and the odd addition of the word 'woman' to the literature. Similarly in university courses, books about women were added to book lists but the old sexist theories remained unchallenged. Feminists often went along with this: we thought of 'expanding Marx' instead of 'transforming Marx'. Marxist feminist theory therefore suffered in the same way as marxism: no historical theory was developed about human reproduction and the relations within which it occurs. It is here that the gulf between the radical feminist legacy and marxist feminism is widest. Radical feminist ideas have most to offer in that they challenge male definitions of sexuality, rape, 'incest', wife-battering and motherhood from the outset.

The doctrine of forgetfulness

Ideas from earlier phases of the women's movement recede temporarily into the background. This is not due to our poor memories or to the economistic features of the domestic labour debate; things also fade because the women's movement doesn't develop in a straight line but as a reaction to other developments. As a result preoccupations change.

This is a general phenomenon of late capitalism which has been analyzed by the American historian Russell Jacoby in his book *Social Amnesia*.[17] He describes the 'social amnesia' by which books, ideas and theories lose their interest. They have become just as subject to fashion as clothes, cars and furniture.[18] These changing fashions constantly undermine the radical tradition, for although some ideas remain influential (Jacoby illustrates this by the example of developments in psychoanalysis in the United States), the critical dimension of these ideas and theories is lost. This explains comments recently directed at the women's movement. Increasingly we hear remarks like: 'what are you nagging about, we know that already, you're always going on about the same thing, can't you ever come up with anything new?', as though anything much had improved in women's situation or in the way it is viewed. Books and ideas about feminism and women very soon have the label 'new' or 'obsolete' stuck on to them and we never ask whether this is justified.

Finally, male-dominated science constantly succeeds in obliterating feminist findings and thus hinders the development of a critical feminist tradition. Mary Daly describes how eerie it is when women who have been lecturing in women's studies for years discover that new students have not yet heard of Firestone or Betty Friedan. 'Old is new, it's as if nothing had ever happened,' sighs one.[19] I have had a similar experience. In a study-group on capitalism and patriarchy which included various politically active women and men, many had heard of Millett and Mitchell, but few had ever read any of their work.

In spite of a fair measure of cynicism and a healthy dose of paranoia, I am constantly amazed at how recent books, scientific and progressive, still muddle along in the old sexist way, despite feminist criticism which repudiates their premises.[20] This is not really the result of a deliberate male plot, but an indication that men often don't even read what feminists have produced, let alone digest it. Joan Kelly cites a book by Mary Inham, *The Two Forms of Production under Capitalism* which appeared in 1939(!), and which examined production and reproduction. Today we don't know anything about it. It seems that new generations of feminists must constantly make rediscoveries and so building up a tradition is almost impossible. Again and again we bury the insights feminists have made in the past.

New lines

In women's movement circles in England around 1976 the feeling arose that the discussion about the connection between capitalism and patriarchy was stagnating. This affected the growth of theory about the roots of women's oppression. This was partly a result of the turn in the debate on domestic labour, but also occurred because the discussion on psychoanalysis had run aground. Initially the new women's movement sharply rejected psycho-analysis. There was some rethinking after the publication of Juliet Mitchell's *Psychoanalysis and Feminism* in 1974.[21] But because she set herself up as more Freudian than Freud and because she saw patriarchy as merely ideological and eternally valid and universal, her ideas offer no inspiration for the movement in the long term. Worse still, followers of Althusser and Lacan gradually began to take over the debate by using incomprehensible language which confused those who were theoretically less well grounded.[22]

The years 1976 and 1977 were also marked in England by the revival of direct political action in the women's movement. In previous years little had happened at national level. Women had concentrated on local concerns or on consciousness-raising. Then threats to reverse abortion legislation, new sexist immigration regulations and some sensational rape cases, stimulated activity and campaigns on a national scale. In 1977, for the first time in several years, a national socialist feminist conference was held, the National Abortion Campaign managed to settle its internal differences and various local groups opposing sexual violence were set up. This put the discussion on the relationship between 'body politics' and the socio-economic battle back on to the theoretical agenda, and this was reflected in articles, pamphlets, leaflets, workshops and study conferences.

To ascribe the breakthrough to one conference (the Patriarchy Conference in 1976), as some English women do, seems to me mistaken,[23] although various ideas presented there can be seen in later discussions. The paper by the feminist anthropologists Kate Young and Olivia Harris, with its emphasis on the importance of the organization of human reproduction, has proved particularly fruitful.[24] It is not completely original, however, and is based, in my opinion, on Gayle Rubin's analysis.

In the attempts to understand the relationship between capitalism and patriarchy and to break through the duality in the formulation of theory, two lines can be distinguished: continuation of the debate on psychoanalysis and discussions about the relations of production and reproduction. Both lines elaborate the debate on domestic labour, but at the same time they employ old ideas of classical feminists like Millett, Firestone and Mitchell in their attempts at a new synthesis.

Psychoanalysis

The interest of the women's movement in psychoanalysis is not only due to its criticism of psychoanalysis as therapy; psychoanalysis can also help to explain the origins of 'femininity'. Central to this is an examination of the processes through which a biologically female child acquires the social identity (gender) of 'woman'. The diverse psychoanalytic answers to this have been debated since the beginning of the women's movement. In England, this debate obtained fresh impetus from Juliet Mitchell's *Psychoanalysis and Feminism*. Aafke Komter's essay 'Feminism and psychoanalysis', elsewhere in this collection, examines this further.[25] In it she comments that marxist discussion on reproduction often only looks at the reproduction of the labour force, not at the reproduction of femininity and masculinity in each generation, and the network of social relations in which it occurs.[26]

I wish to point out two constantly recurring problems in this discussion. First there is always the danger that writers, through their emphasis on the development of 'femininity' and its ideology, forget to ask why, in any given society, 'feminine' characteristics are socialized. This can lead to the misconception that only 'patriarchy' finds its expression in people's ideas which is a theoretical regression to before the domestic labour debate.[27] Second there are also writers who deny the importance of ideology or dismiss it as 'false consciousness', though ideology is not as material as domestic labour.[28] The most promising way out of this is offered by the work of Nancy Chodorow. For her the development of children towards femininity and masculinity is central, but she connects it to the social organization of the nuclear family.[29]

It may seem that the debate on femininity and women's oppression is abstract or a game for erudite academics. But ultimately it can have political consequences. If you see women's oppression as merely 'ideological' then liberation becomes a question of a change of attitudes or something that changes if the material base changes. If the material base is seen as the main problem then you get the well known pattern of socio-economic demands, job-related campaigns and, in some countries, the demand for wages for housework.[30] If the liberation of women depends on a change of attitudes then you get the well-worn arguments about education and consciousness. These demands although important in themselves, don't do justice to the complexity of women's situation, and none in itself provides an adequate basis for liberation.

Production and reproduction

The second line in attempts to grasp the duality can be found in recent work by English and American feminist anthropologists. Their importance extends beyond the world of anthropology.

It is not surprising that feminists took up anthropological ideas. Anthropological arguments showed that women were not forced by nature to be just mothers and providers. Many used Margaret Mead's work to demonstrate that the concepts 'female' and 'male' were specific to western culture.[31] When female anthropologists proceeded to carry out their own fieldwork, this proved disappointing. For anthropology, just like the other social sciences, has many sexist presuppositions.[32] Thus anthropologists in general easily step from biology to culture. Many anthropologists view women's role in biological reproduction as sufficient explanation for male domination and the division of labour between the sexes. If you accept this, then there are no further questions. Rayna Rapp Reiter, an American anthropologist, says anthropology obscures the issues which interest feminists, but that the equation of biology with culture is unacceptable.[33]

Another stimulus for feminist anthropologists was provided by the selective way women were viewed in marxist anthropologist circles. Works by the French anthropologist Claude Meillassoux and the English men Hindess and Hirst,[34] were excellent spurs for women to develop their ideas. Feminist criticism of anthropology is not directed just at the theoretical concepts which men used, but also questions their fieldwork and other empirical data.

The essay by Felicity Edholm, Olivia Harris and Kate Young, 'Conceptualizing women',[35] broke new ground in considering the relation between production and reproduction in a particular society, and precisely what reproduction means. They distinguish three meanings of the concept 'reproduction' and state that all three are of importance in analyzing society. The first, used by Althusser, is the reproduction of all the social relations of society. To survive, a society must reproduce all its parts. Edholm *et al.* do not object to this use, but point out that it leads to 'functionalism', i.e. phenomena are understood and explained by the needs of the system or mode of production. For example: 'Capitalism needs women's oppression' or: 'Babies are produced for capital because the mode of production needs wage-earners.'[36] In my view Edholm's objection is correct. This line of thinking leads to conspiracy theories in which women's oppression is a contrived affair and various mechanisms are perceived as deliberately malicious. Moreover, this concept of reproduction says little about how the different parts fit together, which parts you can distinguish (most marxist writers never deal with biological reproduction separately), and how you can examine them. I find it an additional drawback that the survival of the mode of production becomes central and that the organization of women's oppression is then ignored. Further, because the reproduction of the social structure is always seen in terms of relations of production, the whole 'sex-gender system'[37] is overlooked.

The second meaning of the concept 'reproduction' that Edholm *et al.* distinguished is the one most of us know through the debate over domestic labour, namely the reproduction of labour power. Usually this is seen as the reproduction of male wage earners by housewives (although some analyses still assume that wage earners do this themselves). But the reproduction of labour power and the maintenance of the economically active population are not the only questions of interest. We must also look at how positions are allocated in that population, and how girls become housewives and boys wage earners.[38]

The third meaning of reproduction is reproduction as biological reproduction. Edholm *et al.* think that most theories are based on the idea that biological reproduction is inevitable, and is not an independent action. So certain fundamental aspects of women's oppression disappear from the analysis.[39] Edholm *et al.* advocate the study of population growth and decline (demography) as independent event, on the assumption that this is not simply decided by economic development, but possibly helps to determine it.

Maureen Mackintosh, in an earlier critique of Meillassoux, comes to the same conclusion as Edholm, Harris and Young.[40] Her conclusion is important:

> No conceptualization of a particular mode of production is complete unless it can account for the reproduction of the people within the system and of the system as a whole. In order to do this, three elements have to be considered: the social relations of production, the social relations of human reproduction, and the method by which the reproduction of the system is ensured or enforced. The form taken by the social relations of human reproduction is the patriarchal relation of men to women which dominates the relations of human sexuality and reproduction.[41]

For her the control of female sexuality and fertility is a way of controlling reproduction, and this control is enforced by politics, ideology and economics. For her the survival of the family in capitalism is not a relic from a former mode of production but the way human reproduction is controlled under capitalism.

The discussion in feminist anthropology is more than a clarification of concepts. It is only possible to speak meaningfully about production and reproduction if they are treated separately. Furthermore, feminist anthropology offers good starting points for discussions on what the division of labour between the sexes implies. Anthropology also offers new insights on the division between public and private. In the women's movement these concepts are used loosely to explain women's oppression. Sometimes they mean the division between economics and the family and at other times they refer to the division of space between women and men. Women's oppression goes beyond these terms and cannot be contained or explained by them.[42]

The trade in women

Gayle Rubin's article fits into both sides of the discussion. Her work has significance for the women's movement so I summarize the most important points of her argument.

Gayle Rubin begins with Friedrich Engels' description of the two forces which determine the course of history. Marx and the marxists, she says, have convincingly demonstrated that the mode of production not only organizes production in the narrow sense, but also organizes human relations. A mode of production is both technical and social organization. Each mode of production bears within itself a sex-gender system, 'systematic ways to deal with sex, gender and babies'.[43] Her precise description of this central concept in her theory states: 'A set of arrangements by which the biological raw material of human sex and procreation is shaped by human, social intervention, and satisfied in a conventional manner, no matter how bizarre some of the conventions may be.'[44]

The 'sex-gender system' includes the sexual division of labour as well as the social relations in which biological sex is converted into women whose behaviour is 'feminine' and men whose behaviour is 'masculine'. In some cultures, (Islam), it institutes the separate spheres for men and women. The system lays down rules about sexual choice and establishes whom you can marry and whom not, and also defines your sexual orientation. It lays down rules for your behaviour both as a mother and as a child.

Gayle Rubin believes that the sex-gender system springs from the family and kinship structures of society. These structures are just as influential and just as historically determined as the mode of production in any society. Here she criticizes marxist debates about women's oppression, even though they include a consideration of domestic labour. 'But to explain woman's usefulness for capitalism is one thing. To argue that this usefulness explains the genesis of the oppression of women is quite another. It is precisely at this point that the analysis of capitalism ceases to explain very much about women and the oppression of women.'[45] This requires an examination of the sex-gender system in its various historical forms. The form varies, so Rubin rejects the indiscriminate use of the term 'patriarchy'.

The term 'patriarchy' came into vogue when the women's movement realized that women's oppression could not be reduced just to capitalism or the relations of production. The concept of capitalism has the merit of defining a mode of production which has specific characteristics, but 'patriarchy' is a general concept unsuitable for distinguishing the forms women's oppression assumes in different modes of production. Rubin wants to reserve the use of the term 'patriarchy'. For example, in the Old Testament men oppress women among nomadic peoples and old men also oppress young men.[46] It is one form of the sex-gender system and oppresses some men too. Women's oppression is, however, common to all sex-gender systems.

For Gayle Rubin the rules about sexual choice are basic to the sex-gender system. The heterosexual norm is fundamental. Heterosexuality is obligatory and female sexuality is restricted. She reaches this conclusion on the basis of a re-reading of the French structuralist anthropologist Lévi-Strauss. He 'comes dangerously close to saying that heterosexuality is an insituted process'.[47] He views social pressure to choose a heterosexual partner as a way of creating and perpetuating economic dependence and reciprocity between the sexes, says Rubin. She regards the suppression of homosexuality and the oppression of homosexuals as a consequence of the pressure on sexual choice that also oppresses women.[48]

Rubin uses psychoanalysis to arrive at a theory about the reproduction of kinship-systems. She uses Lacan's Freudian interpretation to explain how individuals achieve their gender-identity. She sees psychoanalysis as the study of the way in which people are slotted into the kinship-system and what that means for their psyches.[49] Rubin rightly states that the views of Freud and Lévi-Strauss stress that women's oppression is much more deeply rooted than is generally assumed: 'The oppression of women is deep; equal pay, equal work and all of the female politicans in the world will not extirpate the roots of sexism.'[50]

Rubin distinguishes the sex-gender system from the mode of production, which helps us to see the problems we must face when we realize that much 'social theory' leaves women out. It becomes clear that the 'women as added value' principle can't explain it all.

Women's oppression can't be adequately explained in an analysis of the division between public and private, (cf. Zaretsky)[51] or in the term 'the family' (that ultimately consists of two sexes). If we recognize the sex-gender system, and accept its implications, then the conceptual apparatus of much social theory and the relations between its different parts must be overhauled.

Critiques

Gayle Rubin's article appeared in the United States in 1975. Since then various critiques of her work have appeared. These criticisms come primarily from fellow anthropologists for her work is still little known outside that circle.

Edholm, Harris and Young respect Rubin's analysis because she makes it impossible to see women's oppression as biological, and therefore natural, or to put biological reproduction in the same category as other forms of reproduction. But they question whether the kinship system, within which Rubin places the sex-gender system, is not ultimately as functionalist as the earlier argument about biology. It was once said: 'Biology demanded that . . .' while now there is the threat: 'the kinship system demands . . . (for example heterosexuality)'.[52] These authors also comment on the new concepts introduced by Rubin, in particular the sex-gender system and the 'political economy of the sexes'. The family cannot be fully explained using marxist laws of value, they say, but it is going too far to view the family completely separately from the operation of the law of value. They warn that biological reproduction should not be regarded as something unique, for that traps us in myths about biology.

A women's study group in Birmingham thinks that Rubin does justice to the complexity of sexuality and ideology, but thinks you cannot restrict investigation of kinship-structures to what is empirically observable, as Rubin does. They believe that Rubin does not go sufficiently deeply into why certain forms of sexual identity are accepted and reproduced in any given culture. The economic basis of a culture and its demographical and ecological characteristics should also be included.[53] They also find, in my view correctly, that Rubin uncritically adopts the Lacanian interpretation of psychoanalysis to explain how individuals learn to organize their sexuality. Lacan's theory uses biased phallocentric concepts. The result is that Rubin, like Juliet Mitchell, sees the unconscious as ahistorical and non-materialist, and so patriarchy also seems unalterable.[54] The Birmingham group attributes her uncritical use of Lacan's conceptual apparatus to her limited idea of 'kinship', saying that the kinship system makes the connections between political and economic relations.[55] Does Rubin see the mode of production and the sex-gender system as so separate from each other that she fails to see the connection between them? I think it is still too early to say. If the sex-gender system is dealt with separately, that guarantees that the insight it affords is not smothered. It gives more insights than any 'total analysis' in which connections are put forward on empirically shaky ground. The danger of theory for theory's sake seems a real one in the discussion on psychoanalysis and production and reproduction.[56] developed in the second part of this article.

their attempt to relate enquiry and reflection on theory. Historical research is indispensable to further insights into the construction and operation of the sex-gender system. This can help us to understand the connection between sexual oppression and class domination. It is a long-term project, but I share Joan Kelly's optimism:

> Conceived as antagonistic ways of explaining and dealing
> with sex hierarchy, the conflicts between separation, and
> between the claims of sex on the one hand, and race and class
> on the other, are themselves expressions of the nineteenth-
> century conception of two sociosexual spheres. It is this
> conception that feminist social theory is at the point of
> overcoming – not by suppressing such oppositions, but by
> understanding the systematic connection between them.[57]

4. Feminism and psychoanalysis

Aafke Komter

I still have half an hour to outline for you how it looks from the woman's side, if I may put it like that. Now only one of two things is possible: either everything I write is meaningless; . . . Or the new function $V \times (\emptyset x)$ in which the negative relates to the quantor and which is read as 'not all x' (pas tout), means: wherever a speaking being runs over to the women then in the final analysis it is based on the fact of being 'not everything' (pas tout), to insert itself therefore into the phallic function . . . The woman does not exist because – I dare again use this term – she is in her essence not complete (pas tout). (Jacques Lacan in *La femme n'existe pas*)[1]

Introduction

The aim of this essay is to offer an overview of the various viewpoints and theoretical positions in the present debate on feminism and psychoanalysis and to give a feminist view.

The debate on feminism and psychoanalysis is 'interesting' not only from a theoretical viewpoint, but because it also concerns our daily experiences, our feelings towards men, women, children, and the way in which we meet our needs for love and sexuality. This is developed in the second part of this article.

I begin with a short historical survey of the development of the debate; then I shall explain the plan of this essay. The debate was started in the thirties by Karen Horney who was the first to criticize Freud's theory of femininity from a women's standpoint. Together with a number of other analysts, such as Melanie Klein, Clara Thompson and Ernest Jones who made up the 'cultural school', she drew attention to the social and cultural oppression of women to which so little attention had been paid in the mainstream of psychoanalytic thought.

After the Second World War this line of argument was continued by Simone de Beauvoir in *The Second Sex*. She outlined the possibility of a symbolic interpretation of Freud's theory of femininity. She saw penis envy, not as the girl's envy of the boy's organ, but as an envy of the privileges connected with the male sex. In addition to the 'male model' in Freud's thought Simone de Beauvoir also criticizes the way in which the sexual instinct is all determining in his theory.[2]

During the growth of the women's movement in the late sixties, the attack was renewed by authors such as Betty Friedan, Germaine Greer, Shulamith Firestone, Eva Figes and Kate Millett. Their rejection of Freud is almost total. They accuse him of patriarchal prejudice and blame him for justifying the oppression of women with theories that pose as science.

The debate gained new impetus with the publication of Juliet Mitchell's *Psychoanalysis and Feminism* in 1974. She regards psychoanalytic theory as a description of the way in which girls and boys learn to internalize patriarchal ideology in the family. Her determined defence of psychoanalytic theory implies a radical swing away from earlier feminists, who considered psychoanalytic theory an endorsement of the patriarchal *status quo* rather than a description of it.

In her work Mitchell builds on recent developments in the theory of ideology such as those stimulated by the French philosopher Louis Althusser, and on the linguistically inspired symbolic interpretation of Freud made by the psychoanalyst Jacques Lacan.

In marxist groups in the English and French women's movement the debate was continued along these lines. In France we can see the influence of Lacan and Althusser in the work of Julia Kristeva and Hélène Cixous. In the work of Luce Irigaray there is discussion of 'negative' influence. It is dominated by criticism of phallocentrism in the history of western thought, especially in Freud and Lacan. A similar critique, albeit less radical, is found in Hélène Cixous's work. In divergent ways Julia Kristeva, Luce

Irigaray and Hélène Cixous all search for room for the female world of experience.

In England, in the new marxist feminist journal *M/F*, attention is given to psychoanalysis as a theory of the ideology of women and men.

Outside the Lacan/Althusser tradition there is the work of American writers like Nancy Chodorow, Adrienne Rich and Dorothy Dinnerstein. They give a feminist interpretation of Freud's theory of femininity and remove the 'phallocentric' elements. Ann Foreman in Britain and Carol Hagemann-White in Germany are similarly little influenced by the French school. The former tries to connect psychoanalysis with marxism and feminism and the latter attempts a synthesis of feminist and psychoanalytic views.

In the first part of this essay I summarize Freud's theory of femininity and Lacan's re-reading of Freud. Then I deal with the French writers Julia Kristeva, Hélène Cixous, and Luce Irigaray and the English debate as influenced by Lacan. In the second part I shall be dealing with the writers who are outside the Lacan tradition: Ann Foreman, Carol Hagemann-White, Nancy Chodorow, Adrienne Rich and Dorothy Dinnerstein.[3] I try to give a feminist view of the ideas and theories under discussion. My themes are: the relation between theory and practice, the study of family relationships in the reproduction of an ideology of the sexes, and the fundamental questioning of patriarchy. All three themes refer to the possibility of a theory that offers a perspective for change in the inequality between women and men instead of a strengthening of the status quo.

Feminism arose as reaction to women's oppression. It is not an uncommitted intellectual and cultural trend, oriented only towards changing mental attitudes, social norms and values. It is a political and cultural movement aimed at realizing fundamental social reforms in the fields of the organization of reproduction, of paid labour, education, culture, legislation, politics and economics (fields which are interrelated).

Feminist theory relates to this practice. Whether we are involved in politics, economics or in the ideological aspects of this practice, it is of great importance that we do not just keep describing what we have known all along, but that we indicate where possibilities for change exist. Theory and the acquisition of knowledge cannot in themselves be our main concern. Changes in the practice of inequality must be high on our list of priorities.

The possibilities for a theory which offers a perspective for change are found in the relation between theory and practice. This relation can be more or less direct. One extreme is the demand that each theory or enquiry can be used immediately for the movement; the other extreme is so-called 'archive knowledge', facts which cannot be linked up with the action against women's oppression, but are data collected solely because an individual researcher was interested.

The second theme concerns the content given to the concept of reproduction in the family. It is my opinion that we must look further than the reproduction of wage-workers, of the labour force on behalf of 'capital' (and the ideology belonging to it), to the reproduction of the ideology of the sexes.[4]

As a result of a growing understanding that the origin of inequality between women and men lies in the way in which reproduction is organized and in the different functions that women and men fulfil in this, more theoretical attention is being paid to reproduction.

There are different approaches to studying reproduction relations. The first approach focuses on the economic and ideological functions of reproduction in the family for maintaining the organization of production (providing domestic labour for the capitalist system, and the reproduction of a disciplined labour force, and the question of whether domestic labour is productive work which contributes to surplus value). In the second approach, the family is considered as the place where sexual ideology is reproduced, where the basis is laid for the division of labour between women and men and the oppression of women. This ideology not only helps to maintain the relations of production but also maintains the relations of reproduction.

Both approaches supply important insights. My impression is that up until now more attention has been paid to the first (see the theory on domestic labour, the 'domestic labour debate', in England and the Netherlands),[5] than to the second. It is important to theorize about family relationships not only in relation to the productive sphere, but also to investigate the network of relationships within which the reproduction of ideology about women and men takes place.

I propose that patriarchy should be discussed in depth. This is of particular importance to the debate on feminism and psychoanalysis, because in traditional psychoanalytic thinking there has been a strong emphasis on the unavoidable and unalterable character of the patriarchal status quo. Feminists should break through this fatalist thinking by not thinking of patriarchy as immutable and by offering a perspective for change.

Questioning capitalist relations, the other pillar of women's oppression, is a matter of course in left wing circles (where the debate on feminism and psychoanalysis is popular. But the emphasis here is not on patriarchy. Theory should offer a perspective for change. This obtains if it opens people's eyes to hitherto unsuspected, hidden, invisible aspects of inequality, if it questions what seems self-evident, if it challenges traditional ways of thinking, coloured by male presuppositons, if it succeeds in avoiding sterility, unnecessary abstraction and mystification and offers recognizable, living and stimulating insights on the subject-matter. 'Here we are concerned with emotional realities which have so far been discussed mainly in the conservative psychoanalytic spirit of understanding why things must be the way they are, not in the revolutionary psychoanalytic spirit of thinking out how they can be changed.'[6]

Freud and Lacan

Freud's starting point was the original bisexuality of the instincts from which femininity and masculinity developed as a result of social relationships. Freud presumed an original psychic bisexuality with an active male component and a passive female component present in both sexes. The sexuality of the young child is initially 'polymorph perverse' and can move in any direction.

He stated that there is only one type of libido and that is male. He calls the girl, who initially has an active clitoral sexuality, 'a little man'. In the first phase of development, the pre-oedipal phase, the mother is the most important love-object for both sexes. At the beginning of the oedipal phase the girl discovers that she has no penis, which gives her a feeling of inferiority. She reproaches her mother for having endowed her so badly, turns away from her as an object of love and makes her father into the love object. In this process the girl represses an important part of her active clitoral sexuality. The development to 'normal femininity' pre-supposes that the girl transfers the sensitivity of her clitoris to her vagina. At the end of this the girl has transformed the desire to take the penis from her father into the desire to receive a child by him.

In boys the incestuous desire for their mothers causes the so-called castration anxiety (castration as punishment by the father for illicit desire for the mother). As a result of this anxiety the boy gives up his mother as a love object and identifies with the person who has the power to castrate him, the father. The superego (the internalized authority of the father) is now formed.

The girl does not experience castration anxiety (she has nothing to lose) so her motive for leaving the oedipal phase is weaker. Thus her superego is weaker than a boy's.[7]

Freud's theory can be interpreted biologically: the instinctual development and anatomical differences between the sexes are all-determining. A symbolic interpretation is also possible: the theory describes the way in which girls and boys find their place as women and men in the patriarchal order.

Endless debates are possible on the question whether Freud refers to the psychic processing of instinctual development or whether he refers to an unalterable biological process of maturing that comes from within. I think Freud's theory is two-sided. In some of his statements he deals with the inevitability of biological development (anatomy is fate), in others he appears to refer to the psychological consequences of it.[8]

The French psychoanalyst Jacques Lacan distances himself from the biological interpretation in his theory by emphasizing language and symbol in the child's development into a male or female subject. Lacan develops the following theory:[9] the child makes his or her entry into society by inserting itself into a pre-existing culture. Patriachal order prevails in this culture. In language and culture feminine and masculine positions are firmly established. Initially the child forms a dual unit with the mother. The boundaries between the child and her/his mother and the surrounding world are not yet fixed. Gradually the child discovers that the mother is not all powerful and that she has the power to withhold satisfaction. The child discovers 'lack'. This is the basis for the emergence of desire in the child (the desire to develop its own identity, its own autonomy, to become a subject of desires instead of an object).

In the process of loosening the bonds with the mother which takes place, the acquisition of language is a fundamental development in which the split between unconscious and conscious psychological life is created. The most important principle of language is that its elements only have meaning through context: (compare, 'I'll drink another glass' with 'the glass is broken': in the first case wine is being discussed, in the second the glass).

According to Lacan, the 'phallus' plays a crucial role in the transition of the child from the so-called imaginary order (in which meanings are not yet fixed) to the symbolic order (in which meanings and symbols are anchored in language and culture). The phallus is the most important symbol of difference in our language and culture. The phallus symbolizes lack, and indicates what is lacking. The child learns that the mother is not phallic, not all powerful; it acquires knowledge of lack. The child knows the father has a phallus, and so separates him from the original unity with the mother. Through the intervention of the father as 'third term' the child makes her/his entry into the symbolic order. The child's own desire can now grow; the becoming of a female or male subject has begun. By identifying with the possessor of phallic power, the boy obtains the promise that he will later himself be able to possess this power. The girl chooses the father as love object and thus prepares herself for her future position as a woman.

Owing to her relation to the phallus the woman makes a negative entry into the symbolic order. She is excluded. 'The woman is excluded from the nature of things, i.e. the nature of language – women complain enough about this nowadays; they simply don't know what they are saying, that is the whole difference between them and me.'[10]

Even an unobservant woman reader will have realized that the phallus figures prominently in Lacan's thought. The theory contains a circular argument, based on the idea of the phallus as the most important symbol of difference. Women make a negative entry into the symbolic order because of their relation to the phallus; the phallus derives its meaning from the fact that it symbolizes difference; difference is necessary to acquiring a position in language and culture; language and culture are dominated by the law of the phallus; that is why women make a negative entry into the symbolic order.

The debate about Freud's theory (the theory as description of and defence for the patriarchal *status quo*) can also be pursued with respect to Lacan. His defenders will argue that the advantage of his theory over Freud's is that he excludes biological interpretation by his emphasis on the symbolic. But is this a real advantage, if the unavoidable and inescapable character of patriarchy is still central in his theory? Once it was said that women have no souls, now it is said that they have no access to the symbolic order. What's the difference? But let us look at what French and English women have done with Lacan's ideas.

France

The marxist feminist Julia Kristeva, just like Lacan, argues that male and female subjects form as a result of a social process in which the acquisition of language is central. Women, she says, stand in a special relationship to power and to language. They possess neither (here I think Kristeva means that women have never been in a position to exercize an influence on culture and language. Thus women function as a tacit support for the patriarchal order.

The origin of this linguistic deficiency lies in the pre-oedipal relationship between mother and child. On entry into the oedipal phase, the father acts as a representative of the patriarchal order and the narcissistic bond with the mother is repressed. But she always remains and expressions of this can be seen in poetic language. Kristeva argues that this ousted being is the source of annihilation of the objectivizing symbolic language and thus the patriarchal order. She warns against a regression to the pre-oedipal, archaic mother and the illusion of a society without antitheses. It is better to opt for a position of contradiction and permanent revolt against the existing order.[11]

In the Introduction to *Des Chinoises*[12] Julia Kristeva describes how women, precisely because they have always lived in a marginal position, are capable of attacking the symbolic order with its apparently logical and 'objective' thinking. It is not clear to me what Julia Kristeva has in mind for the women's movement: must permanent contradiction be our final aim? And it is curious that although she advocates a position of contradiction for women, she herself has not apparently felt any need to contradict Lacan's thinking, itself a perfect example of the logical, 'objective' product of the symbolic order.

Hélène Cixous is much more critical of Lacan. In her view, western thought is characterized by the fact that it has always created antitheses which are hierarchically ordered (male-female, active-passive, superior-inferior). There is always a conflict between the two poles. The man always has a central position both in philosophy and in literature. The subordination of women is a precondition for the male order. In this phallocentric scheme there is no room for woman as an equal other. The purpose of woman's existence is to recognize him, not to 'exist' herself. The primacy of the phallus is constantly reaffirmed in the hierarchical order of sexual differences in which all value comes from the masculine.

It is therefore necessary, Hélène Cixous argues, to undermine phallocentrism as something eternal and natural. She speculates on the possibility of relations between people based on love instead of on the struggle to dominate and on the acceptance of difference without feeling threatened. Here Hélène Cixous finds herself in the 'danger zone' to which Julia Kristeva referred: the illusion of a society without antitheses. The social changes necessary to ensure a successful ideological attack on patriarchy are not clear from Hélène Cixous' work.[13]

In a discussion with the marxist philosopher Cathérine Clément, Hélène Cixous points out the danger of an expertise which hides one's own lack of knowledge, and the bad habit of assuming that certain concepts are common knowledge – a common feature of

Lacan's school of thought. She describes the bewilderment of a woman not familiar with Lacan's terminology when confronted with something like: 'In no case may women penetrate into the kingdom of the symbolic.'[14]

The most radical feminist in the school influenced by Lacan is the psychoanalyst Luce Irigaray. She examines the possibility of a feminine imaginary world. The genesis of this imaginary world would be related to women having sexual bodies different to men.[15] Luce Irigaray points out that for Freud only the male sex had value. He defines feminine as lack, as the reverse, as negative with regard to masculine. Freud takes the phallus as a point of reference for his theory, and views procreation as the highest aim of human sexuality. In his theory on the development of girls he always reasons towards this goal and develops his reasoning on the phallus as norm.[16]

In another article Luce Irigaray states that it has always been the function of women to be a useful object to men and an object of barter between men. Women are the precondition for the functioning of the symbolic in patriarchy. They can only fulfil this function by abandoning their own right to speak.[17]

Irigaray points out that Freud is caught in a patriarchal power perspective and ideology. Through this the oppression of women is reproduced in the patriarchal order. In Luce Irigaray's view Lacan is equally unsuccessful in going beyond his own patriarchal presuppositions. For him, too, the desire of women is subordinated to the phallic order. Although he bases his ideas not so much on anatomy as on the symbolic, (he replaces the anatomical 'lack' that Freud ascribed to women by a 'lack in language'), the same criticism applies: the phallus is everything, the woman is 'pas tout' and hence excluded from the symbolic order. Luce Irigaray says that Lacan elevates his own fantasy into the level of law and science; everything fits into his 'encircling projection machinery', as she calls it. Nothing escapes the circularity of the law of the phallus and the best way of immortalizing the phallocracy is to define it as circular, to make the other subordinate and thus claim the monopoly of truth over femininity.[18]

Her fierce criticism cost Luce Irigaray dear. Immediately after the publication of her book *Spéculum de l'autre femme*,[19] in which she presents the above criticism, she was dismissed from the University of Paris (Vincennes) where she was lecturing in the Department of Psychoanalysis. Jacques Lacan himself was head of this department. There is a striking similarity with the dismissal of Karen Horney from the New York Psychoanalytical Institute; she was the first woman analyst to criticize Freud's theory of femininity. Both events stink of patriarchy.

Luce Irigaray is also severely criticized by female Lacanians. Monique Plaza accuses her of antifeminism, reductionism, naturalism, 'essentialism' (presupposing a specific feminine essence, the 'being', the 'nature' of women). There is no feminine 'essence', says Monique Plaza, in answer to Luce Irigaray's hypothesis that a feminine imaginary world might exist, symbolized by the shape of female sexual parts (the two labia symbolize the lack of unity of female sexuality); you cannot reduce a woman to her biology and you cannot see her apart from what the social environment has done to her.[20]

Although the argument sounds sensible there is a snag, Luce Irigaray warns, in that questions of the type 'what is a woman?' or arguments for the need to develop a theory on 'the woman' are themselves phallocentric. The typical thing about the feminine is precisely that it escapes from any definition.[21] The 'essence' of the feminine is that it has no essence.

The English woman Sue Lipshitz (see below) also criticizes Luce Irigaray for her 'essentialism'. On the whole I find Luce Irigaray's criticism of Freud and Lacan more interesting than her rather elusive philosophizing about the feminine.[22] Lacan has his own thoughts on the subject: 'Our female colleagues, those "lady analysts", do not tell us everything . . . about female sexuality. They have not advanced the question of female sexuality a single step. For this there must be an inner cause which is bound to the structure of the apparatus of experiencing desire.'[23]

England

Juliet Mitchell was the first writer in England to reopen the discussion on feminism and psychoanalysis from a viewpoint inspired by Lacan and Althusser, with her book *Psychoanalysis and Feminism*.[24] According to her, psychoanalysis contains the concepts with which the origins and development of sexual ideology can be analyzed. In the oedipus complex girls and boys experience those developments through which they assume their place as gendered subjects in a culture.[25]

The problem with Juliet Mitchell is that she is more Freudian than Freud. With pent-up rage, which sometimes causes her to quote inaccurately and interpret wrongly, she fights against all feminists who have dared to challenge Freud's male model. Her defence is not always convincing.[26] Moreover, her approach is strikingly ahistorical. Ideology for her has an 'eternal' character and so she loses sight of historical specificity and the connection between patriarchal ideology and the specific economic, political and cultural circumstances of a given historical period.

Juliet Mitchell's book has stimulated interest in Lacan among a number of English women. At a congress held on patriarchy in London in 1976, Rosalind Coward, Sue Lipshitz and Elisabeth Cowie delivered a lecture,[27] in which they stated that psychoanalysis reveals how women are socially constructed by family relationships. The development of sexuality is determined by whether one possesses a phallus or not. The self-image a girl has in the earliest phase is 'non-masculine'. As a result she initially situates her 'ego-ideal' not in herself but in the other, which influences her later love-relationships. Through the intervention of the third term, the father, the imaginary narcissistic phase is left behind. The phallus symbolizes difference which is necessary for the acquisition of a place in language. The growth of desire is allied to the different way boys and girls relate to the phallus. Because they are 'castrated', women make a negative entry into the symbolic order.

Lacan's 'catechism' begins to sound rather monotonous; what he argues is that women are not men and therefore they are worse off.[28] The assertion is undoubtedly true, but does not really shed any new light on the matter. The Dalston Study Group[29] considered the lectures and asked whether the congress on patriarchy was not itself 'patriarchal'. They complained about the lack of background information, information which is necessary to understand the lecture (a short introduction to the works of Freud and Lacan, for example), and the lack of information on sources. They found this intimidating and mystifying. Moreover they found it insulting to hear at a congress on patriarchy that they, women, make a negative entry into culture (of which the congress is a part!). In their opinion it was the other way round: congresses like that produce a negative relationship to 'culture', and the use of esoteric language resulted in women feeling that they hadn't understood, or were stupid.

The traces of Lacan's thought are also clearly visible in the journal *M/F*. The discussion on 'essentialism' is taken up here.[30] This time Michèle Montrelay, a French writer influenced by Lacan, but a 'dissident', is the object of criticism. She presupposes a female libido which is present before taking one's place in the symbolic.[31] Parveen Adams regards this as an essentialist proposition. Representations are only possible if the female or male subject is formed, which occurs under the influence of the castration complex that makes the representation of lack possible. Here the phallus is a crucial symbol. But there is only one sort of libido – male. No representations are possible outside the symbolic so there cannot be a representation of a specific female libido either.[32]

Although it is regarded as the greatest of sins to associate the penis with the phallus, Adams herself has difficulty here. The genuine organ, the penis, readily symbolizes difference, she says. But the phallus represents lack for both sexes. The problem is not that the girl does not have a penis but that she lacks the means to symbolize lack. Whatever the case, you just have to put up with it if you are born female. Again true, but we already knew that.

In the second issue of *M/F* [33] Sue Lipshitz[34] states that femininity does not exist outside the symbolic: 'But feminist analysts like Irigaray find themselves suggesting a return to self-observation by women, both of their bodies and of female experience as spoken out in therapy, as the basis for the construction of a new theory of femininity. Surely the point is that this cannot be done outside existing categories. Any suggestion therefore that women's experience somehow gains a voice in an autonomous realm susceptible to the correct questions and sympathetic ears must be fallacious.' I wonder if Sue Lipshitz has exchanged experiences with other women and seen that specifically female experiences (the result of social influences and not of a feminine essence or nature) are everywhere? Or has she only allowed the deceiving light of the male theoretician to shine on feminine experience?

Parveen Adams and Jeff Minson go further in their article 'The subject of feminism'.[35] The problem with much of feminist analysis is, according to them, that they view the category 'women' as unproblematical; their basic premise is that of a human essence that exists independently of, and prior to, the social. Essential attributes are ascribed to the category 'women' (tenderness and a sense of community), which stand in contrast to masculine attributes (such as violence and the urge to compete). The political position which follows from this is a feminist separatism in which the female nature is presented as the norm, and according to which social practice is measured. Essentialism and moralism are intertwined. This is obvious, from the talk of male 'power', male 'interests', and in the slogan 'the personal is political'. The mistake is that certain 'values' are assumed when they should be the object of analysis. For example, the basic premise behind the slogan 'the personal is political' implies an 'essential' subject.

It seems evident that women and men have different interests, precisely because they are 'socially constructed'. It is obvious that the subject that has a personal experience is a social product and Simone de Beauvoir showed that female (and male) subjects are not born but constructed. The article by Adams and Minson looks like a new argument for value-free science, but this time from a marxist angle. These women's rigid thinking is borrowed from others, and shows no independence. As a result they confirm that no specific, feminine experience exists. To me it seems a not very fruitful view.

We have seen that the debate in England bears traces of Lacan in a more pronounced way than that in France. Unlike the French women, the personal imagination of English women seems scarcely to have been stimulated. For Julia Kristeva an antithesis seems to be implicit in Lacan's concept that no femininity can exist outside the symbolic; in Hélène Cixous and Luce Irigaray we find an openly critical attitude towards Lacan's phallocentrism. All three writers are searching for hidden, repressed feminine elements, and want to create room for a feminine world of experience.

In the English journal *M/F* the doctrine is strictly adhered to. Any attempt to describe the subject 'woman' as someone with a separate development which is not always dependent on the phallus (instead of as deviation, as negative, and not existing in the symbolic order) is called 'essentialism'. The articles constantly emphasize that it is not possibe to speak or think outside the patriarchal order. These writers deny the women's movement's right to exist. Any right of contradiction is denied to women. Those who point to male prejudice are told that they are not in a position to express this: they are themselves a male prejudice. More refined ideological oppression is scarcely conceivable. Even more remarkable is that Lacan's thought is so popular in circles which call themselves progressive and feminist.

Although Lacan's symbolic 'translation' of Freud could in itself offer points of contact for a theory of sexual ideology, phallic blindness prevents him and his followers from developing such a theory. Critical questions are not posed. For example:

– Is Lacan's emphasis on the verbal, the symbolic, correct? Have the pre-oedipal sensations of pleasure, frustration, pain, no influence on the construction of female and male subjects? Freud himself pointed out (following Jeanne Lampl-de Groot) the importance of the pre-oedipal mother-daughter relationship.

– Why is the phallus *the* symbol of difference? Can't symbols of difference also play a part in the acquisition of language and hence the construction of subjects (the mother's breast, the fact that the mother, a woman, takes care of physical gratification, and so on)?

– Why does Lacan place such strong emphasis on the inevitability of the law of the phallus and leave no room for change, for contrary forces? An analogy would be a theory of capitalism in which attention is paid exclusively to the interests of the ruling class, whose interests are presented as inevitable and unalterable.

– Where does Lacan get his insights into femininity from? (From his phallus, perhaps?)

Bearing in mind the themes outlined in the introduction, we can assert the following:

The relation between theory and practice is difficult to find, especially in English writings. A 'hostility to practice' is perceptible in the distrust of certain feminist writings and practices (feminist therapy) and in the difficult theoretical construction of 'essentialism'. The French writings offer a perspective for change of practice at the level of language, speaking and thinking. It is not clear, however, what social changes are necessary to enable and support such ideological and symbolic changes.

In none of the French or English writings, are family relationships, as the locus where sexual ideology arises, really analyzed. The statement that women, because of their relation to the phallus, take a negative place in the symbolic order, seems to me an insufficient explanation for the origins of this ideology. The relevance of the analysis of Coward *et al.* (see above) lies, according to them, in the fact that the antithesis is pointed out between the way reproduction is organized and recent developments in capitalism, as a result of which ever more tasks are removed from the family. The family is becoming 'superfluous', while its continued existence is vital for the maintenance of capitalism (Juliet Mitchell pointed out such an antithesis in her book). Two years later Rosalind Coward (in the introduction to *M/F* No. 1) seems to relativize the revolutionary possibilities contained in this antithesis. She points out that we must not be blinded by the functionalist argument that the family is necessary to maintain capitalism. If capitalism is flexible enough to adapt to changing relations of reproduction, it is then unclear to me what the theoretical and practical implications of the 'antithesis' are. In any case Coward *et al.* aim their analysis more at the ideology of the family in relation to the sphere of production, than at the role this ideology plays in the maintenance of the relations of reproduction.

The French writers define patriarchy in the form of the phallocentrism of Freud and Lacan, as a problem in their attempts to break down patriarchal ideology in language and thinking. The contribution of the English writers confirms the patriarchal thinking of Lacan and Freud. Women are 'castrated' and hence life is difficult for them in patriarchal culture. They do not suggest how this can be changed.

To summarize, we can say that the French writers offer a contribution to changing the terms of the discussion in that they want to free themselves from the shackles of patriarchal thought. They do not, however, present a plausible *theory* on the way in which girls and boys become sex-typed in the family. The value of their work is more literary and poetic. The theory inspired by Lacan, as it emerges from English writings, seems sterile and abstract. Moreover it is mystifying because it excludes any view other than Lacan's by circular formulations. Thus theory degenerates into religion and serves to confirm the patriarchal status quo.

Ann Foreman

Uninfluenced by Lacanian thought, Ann Foreman attempts a synthesis of marxism, psychoanalysis and feminism in her book *Femininity as Alienation*,[36] 'Alienation' is for her the linking concept between the economic and the ideological. As a result of the division between reproduction and production, which occurred with industrialization, the alienation of the woman has taken on a specific meaning. Her role became more and more restricted, to giving emotional and physical care by the withdrawal of productive functions from the family. The woman has become a being 'for another', a passive instrument of pleasure for the man, alienated from her own sexuality.

According to Foreman, unconscious mental life is the result of the process of alienation in capitalist society. She rejects Freud's and Mitchell's ahistoricism, but goes to another extreme: simply remove alienation, which is the result of capitalism, and the unconscious disappears.

I think that Freud's discoveries of structures such as the unconscious and the conscious, and processes such as defence mechanisms in our psychic life, could well have universal validity. Psychic life is dependent on the culture, the social class into which one is born, as well as sex and race. It seems probable that the unconscious as a mental structure will disappear as a result of the abolition of alienation (if it is at all possible to abolish it).

Another unconvincing aspect of Ann Foreman's book is the

idea that the oppression of women only began with capitalism,[37] whereas patriarchy, as we know, is much older than capitalism and women's oppression occurs in non-capitalist societies too.

Carol Hagemann-White

In Germany, Carol Hagemann-White has investigated the relation between feminism and psychoanalysis.[38] In her view power over a thing, over yourself, is a necessary part of desire. For girls power is possible by participation in male power; albeit 'as a victim'.[39]

Nancy Chodorow

Nancy Chodorow's book *The Reproduction of Mothering*[40] represents an important theoretical renewal in the debate on feminism and psychoanalysis. In my view she is the first to succeed in developing a theory about the origins of the ideology of inequality between the sexes, using basic concepts from Freud's theory but without falling into 'phallicism', or patriarchal prejudices.

Women's 'mothering',[41] the fact that women look after children even when they are older, has always been understood in the social sciences as a natural consequence of women's capacity to bear and suckle. Mothering is also a capacity that is reproduced in family relations but this has always been overlooked.

Although there are many variations in the division of labour between the sexes and family structure in different cultures and historical periods, the fact that women do the mothering is a nearly universal phenomenon. The division between reproduction and production is a relatively recent development. As a result the modern family arose as the place where people (men) can recover from work and can find personal fulfilment.

Production and reproduction influence one another; the economic system is dependent on women in the family reproducing specific types of labour.[42] Not only is the labour force reproduced in the family but also the ideology which defines women and men. This is linked to the division of labour between the sexes and the social inequality of women and men.

According to Nancy Chodorow, the fact that women do the mothering cannot be explained by socialization theories, based on conscious learning of the female role and identification with a female role model. Mothering demands an emotional relationship with the child. It is clearly a psychologically based activity and not just the carrying out of certain chores such as keeping the child clean and feeding it. The emotional relations inherent in mothering are, according to Nancy Chodorow, built into the psychological structure of women. In her view, psychoanalytic theory offers a better explanation for this than socialization theories which are oriented more towards behavioural attainments. She regards this theory as an analysis of the family structure and the reproduction of the division of labour between the sexes within the family.

She joins a specific tradition in psychoanalytic thinking, the theory of 'object relations'. In psychoanalytic terms 'objects' are people, aspects of people or symbols of people. In the theory of object relations, sexual urges and their consequences for psychic life are not as important as social relations within the family. Very early social relations determine psychological development and personality formation. For Nancy Chodorow too the innate urges influence the development of behaviour in a predetermined way though the maturing of erogenous zones (oral, anal, genital, cf. Freud) is less important than the influence of the relations between parents and children which affects the way children experience their psychic selves, their sexuality and their personality.

The most fundamental contribution of psychoanalysis is in demonstrating the existence of unconscious psychological processes and how they work. Threatening, painful and frustrating experiences are banished from the conscious. The unconscious is ruled by the laws of the so called 'primary process' which transform unconscious affects and ideas. People use unconscious defence mechanisms as a reaction to fear, dependence and the like. (For example, internalization of 'objects': a child feels safe because it has internalized a protective image of the mother; projection: the assumption of a characteristic in others which is in fact a characteristic in yourself). Psychoanalysis also studies the development of psychic structure. The psychic life of the child is initially undifferentiated (i.e. forms a unity with the outside world, and there is no division between ego and environment). It gradually differentiates from the environment as a result of experiences of fear and frustration.

Nancy Chodorow thinks that the family structure in which women do the mothering has a profound influence on unconscious psychic structures and processes in girls and boys. The earliest experiences of pain and fear, and also pleasure, occur in relation to the mother. The child who initially has a narcissistic relationship to reality (the self is not yet distinguished from the environment), is sooner or later disappointed in his or her expectations of primary love. A so-called 'reality principle' comes into effect in which the child realizes that the mother is a separate being with her own interests and activities.

In this initial psychic development, the differentiation of the self and the first feeling of identity, the father is less involved than the mother, because in most cases he has a smaller share in the primary socialization of children. The first contacts with the father are often in the context of jealousy and form an experience of the 'self-in-opposition'.

The first differences in development between girls and boys are in this pre-oedipal mother-child relationship, which is still largely pre-verbal (according to Lacan, the differences arise only in the phase of language acquisition).

The relationship of the boy to his mother is rapidly coloured by the mother experiencing him as 'sexually different'. (I think Nancy Chodorow means not that the little boy has a penis, but that the mother transfers to her son her attitudes and the expectations of men in general.) This can give their relationship a sexual undertone. Because the mother approaches him as 'other', the boy is stimulated to free himself and to define his own boundaries. He does this by a strong repression of his very first feelings of love for his mother.

Mothers do not experience their daughters as separate from themselves, the primary identification and unity of girl with mother is therefore stronger. There is a 'double identification': in the relationship between mother and daughter the mother experiences a new relationship with her own mother.[43] So girls experience themselves as less 'separate', their 'ego-boundaries' are less sharply defined. Because of this primary bond, the pre-oedipal phase lasts longer in the girl than in the boy, and she never totally relinquishes her first love-object, the mother.

During the oedipus complex the boy represses love for his mother and identifies with his father. Children of both sexes associate mothers with dependence and a lack of autonomy. The boy has the advantage of a 'superior' identification because of the superior position of men in society.

In this same period the girl abandons the mother as love-object and directs her love to her father. The unavoidable disappointment the girl has experienced in relation to her mother motivates her to turn towards her father who can help her to escape from the mother. The emotional relationship with her mother, however, still remains important for the girl. She adds her father to her primary object-love.

The repression of pre-oedipal love for the mother is stronger in boys than in girls. For a boy, oedipal love for the mother is an extension of his former intense bond with her and forms a threat to feelings of independence which his mother stimulates in him at the same time. Boys have to define their boundaries more emphatically and therefore repress the pre-oedipal feeling of self-in-relationship and those qualities which they regard as feminine in themselves more strongly. The rejection of the feminine is a part of the male identity.[44]

In the self-definition of girls the denial of pre-oedipal feelings is not so strong. They emerge from the oedipal phase with a feeling of self-in-relationship, a basis for 'empathy'. For Nancy Chodorow the interest of the Oedipus complex lies in the forming of a different 'relational potential' in girls and boys. Furthermore, it is important that girls identify with their mother through a continuous personal relationship, while boys get to know the male position in its absence. Boys do not identify with the total personality of the father, but with aspects of him. They experience what is called a positional identification.[45]

Nancy Chodorow points out some of the results of this development (which is reinforced by subsequent more conscious learning of sex-roles) for later relationships between women and men. Girls never totally give up their first love, which is why men often remain emotionally secondary for them. They are often at the same time physically oriented towards men. Added to this boys grow up with the rejection of the need for love, so that they often find it difficult to meet the emotional needs of women. The emotional needs of women and men are therefore often incompatible.[46] 'Heterosexual' women look elsewhere for emotional satisfaction – in personal relationships with other women or by having children. So, according to Nancy Chodorow, women's mothering reproduces itself.

Nancy Chodorow describes in her book how the ideology of male superiority is reproduced in the family. The preparation for men's participation in the world of work and achievement and for their smaller emotional contribution to family life, takes place here. The ideology about women and the way in which they are treated in the labour market derives from their function in the family and their involvement in personal and affective bonds. So, the ideology of inequality between the sexes is reproduced in the family. This inequality can never be abolished, unless the reorganization of mothering becomes a political aim of the women's movement.

Nancy Chodorow has a critical attitude towards Freud. His whole theory is constructed around the male genital (penis envy, castration complex, the one male libido, the clitoris as a 'male' organ, etc). She criticizes Freud's 'goal-mentality', his idea that the separation between the sexes serves biological reproduction (this emerges from his use of language: the 'task' of the Oedipus complex, the girls 'must' give up clitoral activities to attain 'normal femininity'). 'Anatomy is fate' for Freud, in a functional sense. So, he appears to give a description of patriarchal culture, then goes on to endorse the desirability of women's inferiority. Even Freud's concept of original bisexuality is coloured by his belief in sexual 'normality'. Children are not originally bisexual, but their sexuality is directed to a woman, the mother.

In her book Nancy Chodorow has begun the type of analysis recommended by Burniston *et al.*, in their excellent review article on feminism and psychoanalysis:[47] 'What is more needed, is the necessary task of tracing, concretely, the relationship between historically specific forms of sex gender identity (including their unconscious representation), the material practices which structure the acquisition of that identity (. . .) primarily the mode of kinship/familial organization, and the organization of economic and social relations which constitute the mode of production.'

Adrienne Rich and Dorothy Dinnerstein[48]

The books of Adrienne Rich and Dorothy Dinnerstein are written in the same revolutionary spirit as Nancy Chodorow's. Nancy Chodorow's book offers the most elaborate theory; the other two are of more literary value.

The three books belong together because all three writers are convinced that the institution of motherhood plays an enormous role in the reproduction of social ideologies. Patriarchy cannot survive without it and so motherhood is presented as natural. In all three books you find the view that so long as women look after children, sons will grow up with a 'double image of women': the woman as helper, someone who gives affection and security and the woman as inferior and hostile (i.e. the madonna and the whore). 'A plain fact, clearly spoken by a woman's tongue is not infrequently perceived as a cutting blade directed at a man's genitals.'[49]

All three writers discuss the complex identification of the daughter with her mother, a relationship full of ambivalence, hatred, guilt and love. The writers share the opinion that to defeat patriarchy men must begin to involve themselves in 'emotional work'. That implies we have to find a different way of loving them, says Adrienne Rich.

This means, among other things, that we cease praising and being grateful to the fathers of our children when they take some partial share in their care and nurture . . . It also means that we cease treating men as if their egos were of eggshell, or as if the preservation of a masculine ego at the expense of an equal relationship were even desirable. It means that we begin to expect of men, as we do of women, that they can behave like our equals without being applauded for it or singled out as 'exceptional', and that we refuse them the traditional separation between 'love' and 'work'.[50]

Conclusion

Ann Foreman sees the relationship between theory and practice, but the root of evil appears for her to lie in capitalism rather than in the interweaving of patriarchy and capitalism. She gives scant attention to the way sex ideology arises in the family and concentrates on the abolition of women's alienation through the destruction of capitalism. Nevertheless she has written a lucid book in which psychoanalytic theory, marxism, the history of the family and the discussion on domestic labour are summarized in a succinct way.

The American writers Nancy Chodorow, Adrienne Rich and Dorothy Dinnerstein examine the way in which sexual ideology in the family is constructed and reproduced. They are inspired to a greater or lesser degree by psychoanalysis, which they manage to purge of patriarchal elements. They focus on and expose the universal 'blank spot' in the social sciences with the recognition that women's 'mothering' is a structural characteristic of family organization.

It is patriarchal to say that mothering is a natural task for women. Many men will not openly admit they agree with patriarchy, but they betray a great resistance to change, precisely in the sphere of reproduction and in everything connected with mothering, caring, or housekeeping. From our experience we know how poorly motivated even progressive men are to changes in this area. In theoretical work there is also 'resistance' to studying the influence of family organization on sexual ideology.

Nancy Chodorow has stripped the Freudian framework of its patriarchal premises and given it a living, human content by emphasizing the nuances, the 'tone', the subtle undercurrents in relationships between parents and children. She has also sorted out Freud's notion of 'parental innocence': parents and children influence one another, and parents also approach their children in a way which is coloured by their own sex.

Adrienne Rich and Dorothy Dinnerstein further develop the idea that woman occasions the first experiences of disappointment and also of intense well-being in the child. This has important consequences for the emotional lives of women and men, for their fears and uncertainties, as well as on general ideology about women and men.

Nancy Chodorow, Adrienne Rich and Dorothy Dinnerstein choose the practice of ideological and social inequality between women and men as the point of departure for their theory. Their theory contains insights that can contribute to how we fight women's oppression because they identify where change can occur: in the organization of reproduction and in the way mothering is exclusive to women. Such a change can only really contribute to women's liberation if it is accompanied by far-reaching reforms in the organization of unpaid and paid labour, the division between work and free time, education and welfare policy. The women's movement has made such a re-organization of reproduction into political strategy, as evidenced by demands for crèches, changes in schooltimes, shorter working hours and the right to control our bodies.

Nancy Chodorow analyzes the structure of the family in relation to the emergence of sexual ideology and its function for the maintenance of the relations of reproduction. Women and men, she says, develop different 'relational potentials', and the ideological anchoring of the different needs in the psychic structure of women and men guarantees the continuity of the family structure over generations.

The last three writers attack patriarchy at its core; the family in which women 'mother'. They want the abolition of the division between reproduction and production, between 'love' and 'work', between the personal and the political. Their books are good examples of the effort to close the gap. They point to the revolutionary possibilities of a situation in which caring and mothering are just as natural for men as for women. 'They cannot be our brothers until we stop being their mothers: until, that is, we stop carrying the main responsibility – and taking the main blame – for their early introduction to the human condition.' (Dorothy Dinnerstein, *The Mermaid and the Minotaur*, p. 90)

5. 'The Policing of Families'

Selma Sevenhuijsen and Jolande Withuis

> The doyennes of intellectual fashion castigate unmercifully those unfortunate enough to have been caught hobbling along in their cast-offs. The latest piece of intellectual haute couture from Paris is paraded in the full knowledge that it is beyond the reach of most of us. Or, to change the metaphor, the dreadful heresies of humanism, functionalism, historicism, idealism, sociologism and so on, are hunted out with inquisitorial zeal. And anyway, how much do these changing intellectual fashions really signify? The cult of Althusser, after all, was started by those theoreticians who now most savagely dismiss him.[1]

In academic circles, and in the women's movement, Jaques Donzelot's book *The Policing of Families*, which was published in France in 1977, is enjoying increasing renown. Some praise it highly, others are less enthusiastic.

The Policing of Families[2] covers a field of theory and practice familiar to feminists: family relationships and their formation by 'intervening' agencies and the relationship between the family and the state. For those readers with a good command of the jargon, the book is a compelling descriptive history of diverse subjects ranging from population politics and eugenics to protective societies for children and the rise of welfare assistance, all based on psychoanalysis. All are analyzed from a perspective of discipline and power.

The book appeared just when progressive circles within the social sciences were beginning to recognize insights from women's studies. Feminist disappointment with marxism has affected left wing men. Explanations starting from the reproduction of a social order defined as capitalist, have been found wanting, not only when it comes to an analysis of the family and the repression of women, but also in psychiatry, family welfare and welfare work. Left wing scientists, eagerly searching for broad definitions, may at first sight find exactly what they are looking for in *The Policing of Families*. It is an interdisciplinary analysis of the relationship between welfare agencies, the family and the state, which is based on historical change and presented explicitly as an alternative to the marxist approach to the family.

We must take a critical look at what Donzelot really has to offer. Is his book a step forward from feminist analyses of the same subject, and do his ideas on family formation, on the relationship between interference in families and power relations at home help us advance at all? Is his theory on power and disciplining better than feminist insights into the same subject? Or does *The Policing of Families* 'take over' the areas and the relations we have discovered, while stripping them of their feminist significance?

Donzelot's book fits into a broad intellecual tradition, currently influential in academic circles as well as outside them. This brings the French philosopher Michel Foucault and the American historian Christopher Lasch into the picture. This article only deals with them obliquely. Both deserve more extensive treatment from a feminist. Here only the political significance of their ideas will be looked at for their 'use' invites criticism.

Backgrounds and method

The Policing of Families has two themes, which makes the book difficult reading. We start with Donzelot's theory, his view on reality and on the historical process, his way of thinking and analyzing – what is called 'new French thinking'. Donzelot leans heavily on Michel Foucault's theories.[3] Second, there is historical research which provides Donzelot with material to support his theory. He fits into the genre of family history: Ariès, Laslett, Shorter, Zaretsky, Lasch[4] – although they all differ greatly. I shall return to the connection between Donzelot and Lasch later.

Deleuze states in his foreword,[5] that Donzelot examines the birth of 'the social', a new area. This coincides neither with the economic, nor the legal. 'The social' came into being at the end of the eighteenth century and the beginning of the nineteenth century and derived from a number of 'mutations' – small lines of development which led to a change in the public-private relationship. The family is where this relationship has most importance, but Donzelot had no desire to write a book about 'the crisis of the family'. He wanted to show that both 'the social' and today's 'liberal' family have the same political roots. What those may be is left open – a vagueness which coincides with Donzelot's way of working; for we are concerned here with mutations and transformations, mechanisms and strategies.

Donzelot appeals specifically to Foucault's theories. Foucault's concept, 'biopolitical', is said to have succeeded in determining those practices responsible for the transformations which result in the modern family and hence bridges the gap between politics and psychology. 'Biopolitical' means the dispersal of political technologies which are let loose on health, bodies and lifestyles. The technologies 'control', but not in the everyday sense limiting, forbidding, repressive, but disciplining and normative, a method of intervening in demography.

This is the 'positive' power of 'the social'. Control of the population takes place through intervention in families. For this reason and in order to show the mechanisms of that control, Donzelot examines the development of family as it took place between the Ancien Regime (which came to an end when the French revolution replaced absolute monarchy with a bourgeois republic) and the present.

Donzelot's work centres around the mechanisms of discipline of the family. He wishes to distinguish himself, on the one hand, from classical nineteenth-century political schools of thought and their vision of the family, and on the other hand from the historians of the family such as Ariès. His main questions also make it clear that Donzelot's motives for examining the developments around the family differ greatly from feminist examination of the differences between the sexes inside and outside of the family.

Donzelot reproaches the historians of the family. He thinks that they have been too concerned with the family as a separate, especially cerebral, social sphere, 'private' and unconnected with economic and other social developments.[6] Their work is said to demonstrate that the bourgeois type of family spread slowly to other classes in society. At the end of the nineteenth century, according to Donzelot, there were two, contrasting, political views. Conservatives and liberals were defenders of the family, for they saw it as a way of perpetuating control over property. Those who attacked the family, (utopian) socialists and anarchists, did so because of that function; and indeed, believed that under socialism, the family would disappear. This view disappeared at the beginning of the twentieth century as the family became a valuable haven for workers, part of 'the quality of existence' and therefore something to be defended. But, Donzelot wonders, how did the lower classes come to adapt themselves to bourgeois morals, to the family way of thinking? How did the 'modern family' become the place where interference in people's lives takes place?

Donzelot wishes to escape what he calls the mistakes of previous approaches. These include the 'political', in which the family is seen merely in its function of reproducing a certain (in this case capitalist) type of society. Engels and Zaretsky both use this approach. Donzelot does not directly relate his history of the family to social economic developments such as that of private property and the state, nor to the consequences of industrial developments. On the other hand, he is also critical of any history of the family which considers the family as an isolated little world.

According to Donzelot, in an analysis in which the family is seen mainly as a reproductive apparatus of the existing order, changes such as divorce laws and rights gained by women can be interpreted only as crises in the bourgeois family or as the expression of contradictions between movements and the 'demands of reproduction'. Concepts such as crisis and contradiction which feminists also use, have become inadequate, because they leave aside fundamental transformations. They concern an outmoded debate in which 'positivity and effectiveness' of the transformations described by Donzelot are neglected, and 'because they lead one in the end to mistake for decisive breaks what is in fact the emergence of new techniques of regulation'.[7]

Donzelot is applauded by Christopher Lasch: 'The best thing is

[. . .] that he refuses to be pinned down by the sterile debate between the protectors of the family who dream of reinstating patriarchy in its original form, and the feminist-socialist-psychiatric critics of the family. He realizes that this debate is finished and his book explains why.'[8] Donzelot attacks marxists and also aims explicitly at and against feminists. We are accused of falsifying history, and Donzelot assumes that real history does not interest us because it might turn out to be more complicated than mere male domination.[9] A weighty accusation. Nowhere does Donzelot substantiate his mighty phrases, and, what is worse, he does not even trouble to quote a name or a title which exhibits such 'feminist' practices.

Donzelot's book also aims at the psychoanalytical movement, because its practice was one of the methods by which 'the social' came into being. Here, Donzelot and Deleuze use the word 'floating' to characterize the public-private relationship – like currencies whose value is no longer fixed against a standard, but depends on the market. Donzelot maintains this is where psycho-analysis plays an important part. Where once a fixed legal system clearly regulated the relationship between the state and the family (as, for example, under the Ancien Regime), a gradual friction developed with legal psychiatry. This friction was solved[10] by psychoanalysis: 'the social comes into being with a system of flotation, in which norms replace the law and regulatory and corrective mechanisms replace the standard.'[11]

Critique

We read Donzelot with mixed feelings. His book is exciting and amusing and sometimes offers new insights or information, but it also irritates and annoys. Partly because his book often seems to be in line with feminist analyses, it is not easy to pinpoint just what is lacking.[12] One cannot reproach Donzelot for not distinguishing between the positions of men and women in the family, whereas so many other writers have failed to do so. Indeed, he examines the question of power and the contradictions between women and men. Our criticism is concerned with his style and with the consequences of his approach to interventions in families. His is science from the male standpoint.[13]

This bias became clear in two ways. First, it emerged from our close examination of Donzelot's explicit statements about women, referring to power relations between the sexes, about patriarchy and feminism; statements which we compared with feminist statements on the same subjects. Second, it became obvious from our search for Donzelot's 'blind spots': all those places where he is wide of the mark exactly because he ignores differences between the sexes. There are innumerable passages in the book which concern 'the family' or 'parents' but where the word 'mother' or 'father' would be appropriate. 'Children', apparently, are neuter as far as Donzelot is concerned, a bad oversight in training and education, for these are so often aimed at preserving gender-identity. Myths of 'universality' prevent insights into many phenomena and developments.

Some remarks on Donzelot's scientific method are necessary as well as a feminist critique. It is not the main target of our criticism, but we feel that its deficiencies cannot go unmentioned. Donzelot offers no more than a minimum of empirical proof for his allegations, while his lack of references renders his arguments practically unverifiable. He excels in vague expressions and general descriptions. He fails to define concepts and is inclined to use confusing labels. His leaps in time are sometimes so arbitrary that we suspect him of selecting events to confirm his views. Such scientific slovenliness hinders an exact comparison other than with the French experience, which is the starting point for Donzelot's theory. This is probably why the reader is sorely tempted to distil so-called truths from the book, making of it a general theory on the relationship between family, state and disciplining.

Donzelot and the family

The family is the starting point and the nucleus of Donzelot's book. Two preliminary remarks are needed in order to make a comparison with feminist approaches to the family. First, we must realize that Donzelot's study of the family takes place within the framework of a wider aim: unravelling power strategies and the functioning of power. He follows Michel Foucault in distinguishing between two forms of power: the first works through rules, prohibition and repression, the second (called 'positive' power) through norms, disciplining, reward and manipulation of the conscience. The second strategy is said to have replaced the first during the past two centuries, and is centred on the regulation of family life. The subject of the 'family' is therefore 'deduced' from theories about power.

When reading the book, one continually wonders where the strategies came from, in whose interest they were, and whether there was a power struggle at all. Did those invested with power derive that power from a dominant position? Do they have special sources of power, such as money, or sexual force, the most important male sources of power in marriage? Such questions, inspired by political science, do not fit into Foucault's power thinking. For him it is the functioning of power which must be understood, power as a process. Questions about concrete issues are dismissed as premature and functionalistic. This excludes many problems and questions and forces readers to immerse themselves in the writer's intellectual constructions.

Second, it is important to realize that Donzelot explicitly refutes the expression 'the family' and a 'general' (i.e. valid for different classes in different times) theory about it. He deliberately uses the plural form 'families'. He examines the way in which families change. Positions and tasks change in time and often differ from class to class. This view is a step forward compared to many sociological theories of the family. Donzelot's book is attractive because it emphasizes historical change and gives attention to external processes which 'model' family relationships. And yet this is also the book's greatest deficiency. Donzelot sees families as the product of power interventions. He has no theory about what preceded those interventions. He is therefore often mistaken when interpreting them.

Feminists start by examining sex relationships and go from there to the family. The family is one of the social forms in which female oppression is institutionalized. Gayle Rubin's theory on sex-gender systems forms a starting point for an approach in which both historical change in sex relations and the existence of similar factors in all cultures have their place.[14] In Rubin's view, the family, as we know it, can be seen as a specific West European form of kinship system with its division of labour according to gender (woman as mother/housewife, man as breadwinner), it is where sexuality, procreation and education are regulated. It is where the foundations are laid for male and female gender identity and for the norm of heterosexuality. Man's power over woman is consolidated in the rules and regulations.

The way in which families are influenced and norms are given, the way in which experts lay down 'rules' or in which the state hands out regulations, can be examined as part of the sex-gender system but may never be viewed as gender neutral. It is not families which are disciplined, but the men and women living in them. This is achieved by a specific division of labour and power relations. Donzelot speaks of disciplining families by birth control. But one cannot say anything sensible on this subject without referring to the disciplining of woman's body or the feminist struggle for the freedom of reproduction.[15] The triumph of gynaecology over women's tradition (old wives' remedies) receives no more than a passing reference from Donzelot. So a whole field escapes his notice. To cover it would have undermined his theory on power in the home.

Barbara Ehrenreich and Deirdre English describe the important role played by gynaecologists in nineteenth-century America in adapting women to male sexual needs. They were deemed to find fulfilment in pregnancy and motherhood. Doctors defined women as sick or hysterical without considering whether their illnesses could be symptoms of their oppression or even resistance to it.[16] Donzelot misses the point because he interprets hysteria as a discovery of criminal psychiatry and therefore he sees the hysteric as 'he'. He should know that hysteria was originally a women's ailment. The concept 'biopolitical' or 'the control of bodies' is new compared to marxist traditions in which people as bodies (or as souls) do not play an important role. But in failing to distinguish between male bodies and female bodies, it is a step backwards compared to feminist insights on body politics, which emphasize patriarchal control over female sexuality and female reproductive power.

Male power, female power
As we have said, Donzelot considers differences between women

and men in the family, but only when it suits his purpose. In his theory, woman appears as a pawn in disciplining strategies. From the eighteenth century onwards, women had to 'tame' their men and children by introducing hygiene and domesticity and by forcing members of the family to spend their free time at home instead of in bars or in the street. Donzelot himself asks several times why such disciplining strategies were successful. An important part of his answer is: because women received something in return. Unfortunately in different places in his book, he defines that 'something' differently. Where the success of hygienic interventions by philanthropy is concerned, women are said to have got 'the opportunity for greater autonomy from patriarchal authority in the family'.[17] But in his Introduction, Donzelot states that women's support was gained because of changing power relations between women and men in the family: women gained power at home, and this was a stepping stone to the recognition of their political rights.[18] Elsewhere he refers to the 'liberalization' of relationships within the family through easier divorce laws. The possibility of the state depriving parents of authority through child protection regulations is balanced, according to Donzelot, by greater freedom in the marriage contract.[19]

In itself, the observation that women co-operated in the construction of family and motherhood is not strange (although Donzelot systematically misses all forms of resistance or deviations from the norm). It would be incorrect to perceive women as unwilling victims. But Donzelot's argument that women are not victims does not take us further. We have a number of objections to his use of the concept 'power'.

Donzelot sees power relations at home as a process of addition and subtraction – what he loses, she gets. Nothing could be further from the truth. Household and motherhood gave women their own world, but just how autonomous were they within it, and didn't this autonomy depend on patriarchal authority? Even if you call autonomy 'power', you must realize that this is a different 'power' from that of men at home, or the collective power of men over women. Men take the most important decisions in the family. For years this was supported by laws and in beliefs such as 'the man is the head of the family' and in the civil laws that prevented women from acting independently.

As the pivot of family life, women have some influence over their husbands. It does not follow that this is 'power'. And it certainly does not follow that this sort of power improves their position or increases their liberation. Recent research, which looks at the power of women, has shown that women influence their husbands in many ways and therefore influence public life. But it would be incorrect to assume that they therefore have power over men. 'One only has to look at the means of power of which women avail themselves to realize that there is still some sense in sticking to the distinction between informal female power and open, legitimate male power. What could gossip, whispering, talk, witchcraft, manipulation and goings-on with "connections" be otherwise than signs of impotence?' asks Marijke Mossink in an essay elsewhere in this collection, referring to anthropological examples of such research. And Renee Römkens has called women's use of indirect behaviour to reach their goal 'the psychical correlation of their oppressed status'.[20]

Looked at from this angle, removing your husband from a bar cannot primarily be seen as disciplining (Donzelot says this is how women destroyed the independence of the working man!), but rather as an act of conscious self-interest. There is no advantage for a woman in a drunken man at home and an empty purse. Donzelot takes a typically male stand, preferring the freedom of the bar to a reminder of awkward obligations at home.

Neither does Donzelot realize that ideological revaluation and the awarding of status certainly do not mean that women have been awarded real power.[21] Indeed, his book is more a description of the regulations and fantasies of bourgeois ideologues (mostly men!) than a solid analysis of family behaviour, although his language suggests the latter. It would clarify matters to distinguish between attributed power and real power.

Writers such as Dorothy Dinnerstein, Adrienne Rich and Nancy Chodorow have shown that patriarchal culture combines deeply rooted adoration of the mother with fear of her. Infantile fear of woman's omnipotence, related to women's caring for small children, leads to a continual need to humiliate her, to control her and subject her to the power of the husband/father.[22] Donzelot's statement on the disciplining of 'free lads' by women is no more than a scientific version of all the well known caricatures of bossy mothers in law and women wearing pants.

There is little sense in taking an isolated look at power in the family. Women were not given the choice of living outside it. During the period with which Donzelot is concerned, women of the middle classes had to fight for admittance to professions, schools and education.[23] For women of the lower classes, prostitution was often the only way of earning money. Here, the fact that Donzelot more or less ignores social and economic developments begins to tell. On this point his book is a step backwards compared with marxist approaches. They at least start from a historical materialist approach.

The suggestion that increasing power for women at home was the stepping stone to political rights is also incorrect. In their struggle for suffrage, some feminists did indeed use the argument that motherhood was a political contribution. But they were battling against the influential idea that biology and household tasks render women incapable of exercizing political rights.

Patriarchy and tutelary complex

Donzelot neither describes nor defines the concept 'patriarchy' clearly. In feminist circles too, there is no clear or generally accepted definition of patriarchy. Opinions differ as to the usefulness of the concept for theories of female oppression.[24] For feminists it is often a quick way of referring to the power of men over women. Statements such as 'family patriarchy has merged into state patriarchy' sound strange to feminist ears. For we see that the state functions more as an extension of the patriarchal arm than as a means of shortening it. One only has to remember that rape in marriage is not considered a crime,[25] or consider the legal status of the breadwinner.[26]

For Donzelot, patriarchal power has the traditional meaning of absolute; it is the formal legal power of the father over his children. In this sense, a take-over of patriarchal power by the state refers to a real phenomenon. The state has limited the power of fathers over their children by measures providing for a take-over of tutelary authority, for placing children under state supervision and for compulsory school attendance. Donzelot is going far too far, however, when he makes patriarchal power melt away with the rise of custodial measures. This is partly because his information is selective, and partly because his concept of patriarchy, which ignores real power relations between men and women and separates the father-child relationship from the mother's presence, is so wide of the mark. A few examples will make this clear.

Donzelot consistently speaks of 'parental authority' which was limited by laws providing for custodial measures. In the Netherlands, the legal expression until 1901 was 'paternal authority'. The Children's Acts of 1901, which made child protection measures possible, changed this to 'parental authority'. This parental power was exercized by the father, for the legislators were unwilling to encroach on paternal authority in the family. From 1946 onwards, parental authority was exercized by both parents jointly, but the father's opinion carried more weight. This demonstrates how misleading it is to speak of 'parental' authority as if 'family patriarchy' had disappeared. We do not think that the French situation differed from that in the Netherlands.

The nineteenth century was a period in which women had practically no rights in marriage. They were not allowed to govern their own property, nor take any initiative in divorce. Adultery by the woman (not by the man) was in England, grounds for divorce because it could introduce children of strange blood into the family and therefore into the line of inheritance.[27] Married women had no parental authority. If they left their husbands, this often meant they never saw their children again. Julia Brophy and Carol Smart described the gradual change which took place in England, partly as a result of women fighting for their rights.[28] From 1839 onwards women were allowed custody of children under six years of age after a divorce and they could visit their children. During the second half of the nineteenth century more opportunities for divorce were introduced, as in France. (In the Netherlands this did not happen until 1971!)

But it would be going too far to speak of freedom of contract even in the twentieth century. Certainly, if we take into account how the law worked in practice, we see that divorce laws affected men and women differently. A woman whose blame for the divorce was legally established had no right to alimony. In England, an 'adultress' lost any chance of being awarded custody of the children or the parental house. The increased possibility of women being awarded custody of the children was based mainly on pedagogical notions that children need mothers, not on a recognition of women's rights. Indeed, Brophy and Smart conclude that the power structure within the family had hardly altered at the end of the nineteenth century and that the power of the father over his children was not threatened.[29] Giving examples of the application of law, they demonstrate that this state was the situation well into the twentieth century, despite increasing formal equality.

Donzelot also sidesteps the fact that pedagogical interventions, whether or not supported by legal changes, were and are often aimed at reinforcing the role of the father. We know from Ehrenreich and English that popularized psychoanalytic theory in the United States led to fathers being allotted many different tasks in children's upbringing. They had to ensure correct gender identification and also play an active, leading role in children's upbringing. This coincided with the 'discovery' of bad mothers by the experts: mothers who rejected and mothers who were over protective.[30] We cannot imagine why Donzelot has not come across such developments. Now and then he mentions something, but, in view of his gender neutral use of language and his superficial descriptions, he seems to have overlooked a great deal. He mentions rejecting or over-protective parents.[31] He describes a psychoanalyist who wrote worried articles in the 1930s about divorce and widowhood and children under maternal authority.[32] He then stops, and we are left wondering what was wrong with maternal authority, what did people think about mothers and fathers, what sort of remedies were suggested? In the Netherlands the right to association with one's children after divorce leads to the application of legal and pedagogical pressures if fathers are threatened with loss of control over their children.[33] This sanction cannot be understood using Donzelot's approach.

Alliances

The second half of the nineteenth century was marked by a

> decisive alliance between promotional feminism and
> moralizing philanthropy in the dual battle against brothels,
> prostitution and the vice police and then against convents and
> the backward education of women.[34]

With one sweeping stroke of the pen, Donzelot lumps widely
differing phenomena together. He elaborates on this statement by
referring to a book by a philanthropist and a book by a feminist,
both advocating educational training for women in order to
prepare them for marriage. This does not demonstrate the
existence of other alliances.

Kathleen Barry's information about Josephine Butler's campaign against English prostitution laws shows how careful one
must be with such issues.[35] These laws were presented as social
reforms, aimed at preventing the spread of venereal disease and
promoting hygiene. They served to force prostitutes and any
woman suspected of prostitution (any woman alone on the streets)
to submit to a medical examination. If no infection was found,
they received a prostitute's licence. The result was that men, the
visitors to brothels, remained untouched, and legal prostitution
was limited almost entirely to brothels. It therefore became
difficult for women to leave the profession. Butler's campaign
against prostitution laws, originally fought by means of lectures
and petitions, grew into a broad movement. Her arguments were
entirely feminist. She saw the laws against the background of
sexual double standards, as legalization for and formalization by
the state of the sexual slavery of women. In her view legislation
should have been aimed at those who profit from prostitution such
as pimps and against the double standard by which a man visiting
prostitutes is considered normal and male visitors are not
punished.

Eventually the campaign was taken over by 'purity crusaders' as
Barry calls them. Josephine Butler's feminist demands were
gradually overwhelmed by traditional Victorian morality. While
Butler was out to expose the exploitation of all women, the new
movement aimed at protecting young, beautiful, white, innocent
girls, 'female virtue' and the family. What the purity crusaders had
in mind was not the liberation of woman, but the restoration of her

position at home and of Victorian sexual morals. 'What in fact happened was that the social purity movement, by attaching itself to women's causes, was able to build a mass movement and to undermine the goals of feminist leaders like Josephine Butler.'[36]

The importance of examining these differences between the goals, demands and strategies of feminists and purity crusaders, instead of simply talking about alliances, is well illustrated by the prejudiced and mistaken observation that feminists and right wing politicians really want the same thing: a ban on pornography and a return to Victorian morals.

Welfare aid

In the Netherlands it has become fashionable in many circles to ridicule welfare aid workers and therapists. Authors such as Foucault, Lasch and Donzelot help the ridicule along. People are said to be at the mercy of 'psy-technology' as a result of searching for the 'truth' about sexuality, relationships or upbringing. This is then lumped together with 'navel-staring' and the 'ego-era', and the old left wing taboo about psychology is brought into play. Therapists are said to create problems rather than solve them, mainly in order to maintain their profession and their power.

This school of thought assigns divergent roles to feminists. Frits van Well blames the women's movement for the demand for therapy, arguing that encouraging self-examination with regard to sexuality creates a floating border between normal and abnormal. 'The continuous question "what do I really want myself?" produces fear and uncertainty and creates the need for clutching at psy-apparatus which seems to bring relief at the level of psychic-sexual functioning, by producing images and counter-images of normality and abnormality.'[37]

On the other hand, Hans Achterhuis, the controversial critic of welfare work, revels in the contribution of the women's movement.[38] He attempts to place the feminist approach to welfare work and medical care within Foucault's tradition, by stating that feminism exposes repression, disciplining, 'sexist infection' and control over woman's role by welfare workers. He sees professionalism as the root of all evil, a tendency which he spurns in the rest of his book. Indeed, he praises feminist 'alternatives' which centre on deprofessionalization and unlearning expertise.

The women's movement, it would seem, is used by everybody to prove what they want. Some clarity on feminist criticism of welfare aid and on feminist practice in this field, is sadly wanting. The statement that welfare aid is repressive or sexist, or that all misery is imagined and requests for help make people dependent is not a basis for any useful theory. We must ask when welfare aid is sexist and what are its non-sexist forms.

Unfortunately, *The Policing of Families* reveals nothing about the sexist nature of welfare aid. This is most obvious in those passages where Donzelot's information is incorrect or incomplete. When reading child protection files, he consistently overlooks the sexist views about mothers which lead other agencies to intervene. We have already mentioned the overprotective 'parents' instead of 'mothers' and his apparent amnesia with regard to women's designation as 'hysterical'. Such omissions flow from his deeply biased view of reality. In our view the concept 'undermining the autonomy of families' is useless and confusing in situations which are primarily concerned with maintaining male power over women and not with taking women's autonomy seriously. The most well known example is when welfare workers persuade women to adjust to abusive husbands instead of making the abuse stop or giving women the opportunity to free themselves from marriage.

Donzelot offers few starting points for thinking about non-sexist forms of welfare aid. This is directly related to the nature of his project, namely unmasking welfare aid as a power strategy directed towards families. In his interpretation of welfare aid, Donzelot is remarkably similar to Christopher Lasch.[39] Lasch's most important axiom is that social developments have taken many functions and skills away from families, and these have been lodged with the welfare professions. Fathers no longer have authority to pass on to their sons, and mothers have become cold and emotionless. So, both the warmth and the secure severity of the bourgeois family have disappeared. Lack of open conflict leads children to be narcissistic.[40] 'Permissiveness' makes everyone unhappy.[41] The process also has serious political consequences.

Lack of conflict means lack of conscience and in turn leads to lack of political resistance. The welfare aid professions are most to blame for this. The patriarchy of fathers has been replaced by a therapeutic state, with a strongly manipulative social control unlikely to meet resistance from an apathetic and dependent population.

In our view Donzelot and Lasch place too much importance on welfare aid. After all, how many people come into contact with it and, if so, allow themselves to be determined by it? On the other hand, they see welfare workers as a uniform group, as willing executives of a repressive state apparatus. Donzelot's views on welfare aid illustrate the hidden danger of his analysis. It becomes a strongly functionalistic conspiracy theory,[42] all disciplining is seen to succeed. Thus many contradictions disappear such as social resistance and internal contradictions between welfare aid agencies. The social struggle for better amenities and legislation also disappears.

One of Donzelot's biggest mistakes results from his emphasis on disciplining and power over people. This leads to a biased interpretation of history and the present. His statements about a gradual change from medical-psychiatric to psychoanalytical diagnoses are made against a background of ever more intervention in people's lives. This is progress compared to medical thinking about innate qualities and to moralistic views which lead to punishment. Donzelot fails to see that some forms of welfare aid help people to regain power over their lives (conquering phobias, gained insight into the source of one's fears, sorrows, incapabilities), or resist power wielded against them (literacy projects or disabled persons' groups). You don't have to be a feminist to formulate such a perspective, but feminism gives it a specific content by developing non sexist forms of welfare aid both inside and outside professional welfare agencies. In the Donzelot and Foucault school of thought, any aspiration to liberty and self realization would probably be dismissed as a new strategy of the power discourse. For expertise equals intervention equals strategy from above equals disciplining equals power. It isn't so strange that men become uncertain when women wonder what they really want from sex. Everyone would be better off if men realized the positive potential of therapy for helping them to deal with fear and uncertainty, instead of inflating their fear of therapy and losing their security in theoretical systems about disciplining.

We do not consider Donzelot's book to be a contribution to feminist theory. Rash statements about power, a flawed concept of patriarchy, careless, forgetful passages about feminism, do not increase our insight into the relationship between women, family and the state. Donzelot's views effectively hide the existence of men's power over women, in the family, in welfare aid and in medicine. His science is a male point of view. By keeping male power invisible he confirms its existence. This sexism in science goes much deeper than merely making nasty or ridiculous statements about women. It is sexism by omission: by not thinking sex relationships through, by asking the wrong questions, by going along with the sexist imagery of one's sources instead of critically examining them, female oppression is hidden from view.

We have our doubts about the scientific and political usefulness of the book. It would be a pity if the need to improve marxism, to extend it to cover the relationship between public and private life – a need which stems partly from the women's movement and its critique of sexism – were to end in Donzelot. We are better off with detailed research, concerned with the workings of agencies and 'sectors' of state influence in specific historical situations, than with the pretentious global theories of Donzelot.

6. Women's struggles in the Third World

Annemiek Hoogenboom and Annemieke Voets

Introduction

In the Netherlands little is known about Third World women. Few groups in the women's movement or the Third World movement are actively involved with women in developing countries. Most of our information on Third World women comes from American and European 'experts', not directly. Interest is growing, however, due to the increasing number of foreign women in the Netherlands, the influence of women's studies in the universities and a growing awareness among solidarity committees that support for women in liberation movements requires independent activity by women's groups within the committees.

Women in the Third World cannot avoid learning about our culture, as it is constantly being exported to them. Our way of life is presented as an example to be copied, particularly our model of the family.

We lack knowledge of one another, so both sides fall back on to stereotypes of each other. We imagine pathetic women, wasted by hunger and countless confinements, totally dependent on husbands, fathers, or sons and severely oppressed, in extreme cases by excision of the clitoris. They caricature our culture and western feminism. Their experiences with white imperialists, colonial education and western TV programmes have given them a picture of a rich, affluent world, free from financial and social problems.[1] Asian and Moslem women feel threatened by the battle for sexual liberation which characterizes western feminism. They dismiss feminism as a luxury enjoyed by manhaters who only want sexual freedom and have no interests in common with peasant women, because they don't experience hunger, poverty and exhaustion. Women who have no access to public life cannot organize themselves in the same way as western feminists.

It is important for the women's movement in the First World to learn about our sisters in the Third World. We can learn a great deal from them. Their oppression is clearer, more 'visible' and often emerges in public, collectively organized practices such as clitoridectomy,[2] whereas our oppression is more subtle and imperceptible. Their ways of struggle can inspire us. In socialist Third World countries women have achieved collective domestic provisions and childcare, on which we can base our own demands.

An understanding of the situation of our sisters in the Third World can help prevent our struggle being misrepresented and exported as development policy. Western 'emancipation', represented as equal legal rights and access to modern education, has been an ideal for women who have traditionally been denied them. This procured diplomatic goodwill for the Shah of Iran in Europe and in the United States for years. India also has legislation in which feminist demands are recognized as desirable. But the discrepancy between such legislation and the living conditions of the mass of the people exposes such emancipation as a sham and in reality serves to increase the differences between women.

A greater knowledge of each other arms us against false appeals to solidarity as women. In parts of the Third World movement and in progressive Christian women's groups a more ascetic lifestyle and a reduction in consumption are posed as the way to help the Third World. Women, who are said to control buying, are exhorted to a sacrificial frame of mind.

Women, both here and in the Third World, all suffer in a world in which there is no equality. The reproductive function women fulfil all over the world affects them more, to the degree in which standards of living deteriorate. Our control over reproduction, including control over women's bodies and sexuality, is most vulnerable to political and economic forces. In the Netherlands unemployment and cuts hit women hardest. In Third World countries an economic crisis means immediate food shortages. In the propaganda of all right wing regimes in the world, women who want to question that being a wife and mother is the 'natural' way for women to behave are depicted as a threat to marital and family happiness and as a menace to the future of their sons and daughters.

In the first section of this essay we describe how women in the Third World are politically and economically oppressed. We trace how western countries have succeeded in dominating developing countries politically and economically. We take a look at how this domination influences the life of women and at the role development policy plays in this. We conclude with a summary about how the situation of Third World women differs from that of western women.

In the second section we look at how women in the Third World are fighting for their liberation in the liberation movements against imperialism. We examine how these movements see the struggle for women's liberation. We look at how women develop mutual solidarity, and what problems they encounter. We discuss women's organizations, whether separate women's organization exists and what this policy means to women. To illustrate the relationship between feminism and socialism we give examples, in particular from Cuba and Mozambique, where women are working actively for their interests within the context of national liberation. Finally we investigate the ways in which the women's movement in the west can support the Third World women's struggle for liberation.

'Development of underdevelopment', is how A. G. Frank, who studied the dependence relationships between Latin America and the West, described the process of the increasing dependence of developing countries.[3] Since these countries were 'discovered', and came under the influence of the capitalist power centres in Europe and the United States, any form of independent economic development has been smothered.

In the heyday of trade capitalism once the most important voyages of discovery had been made, and the rich possibilities of the new regions had been discovered, Spanish, Portuguese and Dutch explorers overran Latin America on marauding expeditions searching for gold, silver and other precious minerals. In Asia and

Africa exploration was initially limited to the coast. Trade agreements were concluded with native rulers. Spices, herbs, ivory and slaves were bartered for weapons. Europeans provoked tribal wars in Africa to keep the demand for weapons constant. Ships transported slaves from Africa to Latin America and on to the south of the United States and returned to Europe laden with minerals. Colonizers first settled in Latin America, where they established plantations for the cultivation of trade crops such as coffee and sugar, when the main gold and silver mines were exhausted.

Africa came under the power of the European mother countries in the nineteenth century. The continent was divided up among the European states with pencil and ruler. Production was concentrated in plantations and mines. Railways and ports were planned to make exporting easy, preferably to the mother country. In Asia the domestic economy was not organized so directly by the colonizers. Treaties were concluded with local rulers and their own political and economic structure was maintained for a relatively long period.

It is important to realize that the now underdeveloped regions were no more underdeveloped than Europe at the time of the rise of world capitalism. The term imperialism was first used in the nineteenth century to describe the policy of Louis Napoleon in France. The term has altered in meaning since then. In general the term is used to describe the creation of underdevelopment and dependence on a world scale by capitalist centres in the west. This underdevelopment shows itself in various ways. Monocultures, dictated by the needs of developed capitalist countries, are typical of regions under imperialist domination. States in Central America had to concentrate so intensively on banana cultivation that they gave rise to the term 'banana republics'. Tropical crops, minerals and raw materials became the most important exports from developing countries. Industrial colonialism led to a total restructuring of the world economy. Colonial societies were organized purely from the point of view of the mother country and its profits.[4] A native bourgeoisie arose in the colonies. They in turn were dependent on international economic relations. The first demands for political independence came from this bourgeoisie.

Latin America became politically independent in the last century, Africa only in the 1960s. Most Asian countries won political self-rule after the Second World War.

Decolonialization and political independence have not changed the system of dependency between and within countries. In many countries the system has intensified. Economic power is still concentrated in the west and administered through multinationals, the twentieth century product of capitalist development. Western states are part of this. Only a few countries in the Third World have managed to struggle free from the international division of labour in which 'some countries specialize in winning and others in losing'.[5] Those are countries where an anti-imperialist liberation movement took the initiative for independence.

The raiding of the Third World has mainly been examined without noticing its effect on women. The emphasis in analyses of imperialism and world inequality always lies on exploitation within production. The struggle for control over reproduction is rarely discussed.[6] We want to show the way relations of dependence and inequality affect women's lives. We are doing this in order to compare the expressions this oppression assumes in various cultures and in different parts of the world, to understand the differences and to develop strategies that enable us to combat oppression in every form it might assume. We look specifically at women's work in agriculture, alterations in family structures and the influence of imperialism on sexuality and on motherhood.

We use examples mainly from Africa and Latin America. We do not go far back into history. We are more concerned with the ways in which the work, spirit and bodies of women are dominated now than with a complete historical survey. The influence of imperialism on women varies according to social class. We do not consider women from the higher socio-economic classes,[7] but concentrate on poor women in rural areas and in shanty towns. In Latin America there is an immense distance between rich women and poor women. Women of the higher classes are the first to ape the western way of life.[8] In Africa the contrasts between rich women and poor women are more blurred, except in the racist South.

Seventy per cent of agriculture in Africa is still in the hands of women.[9] In regions where shifting cultivation was practised –

cultivating a plot of land for a number of years and then letting it lie fallow – agriculture was always women's work. Men did the preparatory work of rooting out trees and levelling the ground and women did the rest, helped by the children. They had to maintain themselves and the children on the results. The remainder was bartered in the market. The cultivated land was communally owned by the tribe.

The arrival of colonizers undermined the position of women as independent farmers and food producers for the community. Men were forced to work on plantations and in mines and often migrated to the cities. Women were left to do the farming on their own. The introduction of private property meant the end of tribal ownership of the land. Men acquired the ownership of this land because they had money for their work and were also regarded as owners and breadwinners by the colonial administration.

The system of shifting cultivation could no longer be maintained. The overworked fields became infertile. Women could no longer keep up vegetable cultivation and were forced to switch to cultivating crops poor in protein and vitamins such as cassava which can be harvested when needed. The result was under-nourishment of the population and exhaustion for women, the beginning of a vicious circle, in which women could achieve progressively less. This resulted in the destruction of women's economic independence and the loss of their traditional power base in the countryside. Their work was gradually viewed more and more as a complement of the men's work, and became so, because they were working on men's land. Their work assumed a private character, working for the benefit of their own families, no longer for the community.[10] This is still the situation in many African countries.

The cultivation of commercial crops takes place on plantations. In rural areas this work is officially entrusted to men. They then in turn put their women to work. New developments in sowing and harvesting methods, improvements in the quality of crops are first tried on commercial crops. Male agricultural and development experts give agricultural training to male farmers. No ideological justification is needed. A productivity gap between men and women results, evident in the contrast between export oriented agriculture and women's subsistence agriculture.

The women's work in agriculture is unpaid, so the wages of the men in the capitalist sector can be kept low. No family or breadwinner wage needs to be paid. Women even send food to their menfolk in towns and because they are often the ones who pay taxes – in kind – an even lower wage need be paid than is necessary for the livelihood of workers. So the 'favourable investment climate' is preserved. The social provisions are kept to a minimum: children, the elderly, the sick and the disabled are supported and looked after by women.

The colonial system also exploited the trading position of women. The distribution of essential foodstuffs was originally dominated by women traders. The existing domestic trade relations were, however, restricted and directed to export. An extensive state and services apparatus was constructed in the urban centres for the benefit of foreign undertakings and foreign trade. This did not raise the local standard of living, but was aimed solely at export growth. The new structure employed men and the services and trade of women were degraded. Women became the primary gatherers of goods and lost their hold on the market structure and hence the rewards for their products.

The expansion of imperialism was possible partly because there was an already existing division of labour between women and men, which could be exploited. Imperialism strengthened this division of labour to the detriment of women. They were excluded from the production of surplus value and went over to necessary production on behalf of the family. This necessary labour involves more than household production in the west, it includes providing water, gathering fuel, agriculture and looking after small livestock.

With increasing job specialization, the dominance of women in trade and agriculture shifted to men. The share in the economy of the independent woman farmer and trader became heavily underestimated and was excluded from labour statistics.

Western norms and values were introduced, with an absolute division between those which applied to women and those which applied to men. Societies in which the nuclear family was more the exception than the rule and something that occurred more in elite circles in the city than among the poor rural population, were presented with the patriarchal family as an ideal. The family was projected as the place where children should be born, and their care and upbringing were attended to by their one natural mother. Polygamy and extramarital sex were declared taboo in societies where they had been usual or at any rate tolerated. Polygamy was condemned but not because it is unpleasant for women to share a man with several women, but because the nuclear family is an effective means of political control.

Men were encouraged to act as the head of the family. Women had to place their life and work at the service of husband and children. They had to become good mothers, be self-sacrificing, gentle and patient. The missions, colonial education, legislation and administration imposed the western model family with its double moral standards, on cultures in which women had never been subordinate to a man, in which they had occupied an independent and economically powerful position, had a certain political power and enjoyed social privileges. In some cases the western family pattern also offered advantages to women, for example in polygamous Islamic cultures. But as long as women in these societies live in isolation, and are excluded from social life which is ruled by men, bonds with other women form a more reliable source of political and economic support than the uncertain support and income from men. Export of the mono-gamous family in itself can reinforce the isolation of women from one another. The popularization of the image of woman as subordinate to man and the limitation of women's freedom of movement had a material aim. It freed cheap male labour for modern production. The discrepancy between the imposed ideal of the family and the reality of life for women and men was, and is, huge, precisely because of the way the exploitation is organized.

The migrant system in southern Africa forms an extreme example of how the existing division of labour between the sexes is used to recruit as much cheap labour as possible. Men are recruited for work underground in the mines or for work in the ports or on plantations preferably when they are already married, have built a house for their family and when it is certain that women will look after the upkeep of the family and the production of food in the absence of the men. Women scarcely ever obtain permission to migrate. They vegetate in the homelands. They keep the local communities together with their labour. Men are more dependent on women for their social contacts, living conditions and food than the other way round. An African community can survive without the contribution of the men of working age, because women always do the lion's share of the work. This makes migrant work much cheaper than a stable labour force.

In Africa and in the latifundia regions of Latin America, where agricultural workers work under feudal conditions, the migrant system has flourished more than in Asia with its intensive rice cultivation. In Southeast Asia whole families worked on tea, sugar and rubber plantations. When the rice planting season drew near, however, the whole family was sent back to its village in order not to endanger the family food supply. Whole families regularly had to shift house. In Africa and Latin America poor families were and are regularly broken up for long periods over huge geographical distances. In Latin America migration follows a different pattern from Africa. The women move to the city to find jobs as servants, while the men stay at home in the rural areas. Agriculture is traditionally men's work and for that reason they remain behind as farm workers on the great latifundias. Women have become maids in such great numbers that Eduardo Galeano calls the whole of Latin America 'the maid who puts her life at the service of others'.[11]

Living the myth of the western family doesn't feed your family. The gap between the western ideal of a family and reality is great in all three continents, enormous in many Third World countries. This makes it impossible to compare the dependence of women in the Third World to that of western women who have their husbands' weekly wage to spend. Where economic insecurity prevails, women are forced to economic independence, for which they often have to trade their self-respect. They become whores out of necessity, or because they lose their traditional work to men through mechanization of harvest and processing activities (as in Southeast Asia in the rice-hulling mills), they are forced to degrade themselves as stone-breakers in road-building. Their dream remains to marry a man who can look after them, as happens in middle class families. Propaganda pictures of a radiantly laughing man and woman, with one child in their arms and another child on their knees, only stoke that desire. But in most Third World countries you can't find that picture reflected in street life.

When women move to the city because there is no longer any work for them in the countryside or because they are accompanying their husbands, there are few opportunities open to them. They end up in slums and overpopulated suburbs in which the possibilities for independence are minimal. In the city, unlike the countryside, everything has to be paid for: rent, food, clothing, transport. They are often forced to become prostitutes in order not to die of hunger. The first female workers in African cities were whores who sold their bodies to Europeans, Asians and a growing number of African city dwellers. Cities from Lourenço Marquez to Havana and from Shanghai to Sao Paulo changed into huge brothels with the invasion of foreign rulers. In Djakarta, Calcutta and Nairobi sexual diseases are one of the most serious problems of public health. For women, old traditions and rights have been lost and replaced only with dependence.[12] Women receive migrant men, supply pleasure with their bodies and then pay with premature decay and disease. Sometimes they hope that by giving birth to a half-white child they will achieve some status. Women in the city stand a high chance of becoming whores. Women in the rural areas on the other hand are tremendously restricted in their freedom of movement. That is why men in Africa and Latin America often do not allow their wives or daughters to go to the city. We have to be aware, however, that where prostitution is common, prostitutes do not have such a stigma attached to them as in the west. In Africa even trading women turn to prostitution as a respectable sideline.

Political and military violence uses the sexuality of women as a constant target in a more aggressive way than economic imperialism. Racism, which accompanies all war, increases sexual violence against women. In Vietnam, French and American soldiers used prostitution and rape to emphasize their superiority as male conquerors and to undermine the morale of the Vietnamese troops as deeply as possible. Imperialism affects women in an even more painful way when their children are mutilated in the womb by chemical warfare.[13] Psychological colonization strategy treats women as part of the spoils of war and this destroys any feeling of self-respect among the vanquished. Women political prisoners become victims of the sexual sadism of their interrogators and guards, who can torture and rape them with impunity, sometimes in the presence of their husbands, fathers or brothers, in order to break down resistance. The use of women's bodies as a means of political pressure, however, often provokes great solidarity among the women who have suffered from it. Female prisoners and women in refugee camps often succeed in supporting one another and bridging political differences under extremely oppressive conditions. They often seem superior to male prisoners.

Humiliation, rape and physical disfigurement are the imperialist price for women. Vietnamese girls underwent plastic surgery, such as the westernizing of their eyes, to increase their market value for American soldiers (the more western, the more beautiful).

The rulers are unconcerned that women provide sexual pleasure for the oppressed. Hardly anything is done to stem the growing tide of prostitution and sexual diseases in the Third World. It is politically convenient that bed prevents people from realizing they are oppressed. Or as the Neapolitans say: 'bed is the poor man's opera'.

The same demands for birth control which are made by the women's movement in the west in order to allow women the right of self-determination over their own bodies, are used in the Third World to manipulate women's fertility.[14]

Population policy has distributed motherhood in such a way that some women gain by it, but many lose. The prevailing idea behind it is that population growth squanders extra production, which leads to greater poverty, so population growth must be restricted. The impact of western family planning is great in Third World countries because western oppression has gradually stolen the knowledge of contraception from women. Women once knew methods of birth control. Migration, the import of foreign culture, religion, education and western medical science, all contributed to the loss of traditional knowledge. Developments in fertility technology mean that human reproduction has become an object of political manipulation and profit. For women, this has radical consequences. A large family frequently becomes the only weapon against poverty.[15] North American missionaries and doctors sterilize women, often unaware of the implications, in empty regions such as the Amazon, Uruguay, Bolivia and Guatemala. 'In Latin America it is more hygienic and effective to kill the guerrilla fighters in the womb than in the mountains or on the street.'[16] In Southeast Asia the coil, condoms and pills vied with bombs and machine-guns in stemming the growth of the Vietnamese population. The same is happening now in Palestinian refugee camps. With a deliberate disregard for health and civil rights, governments and organizations try to dominate the fertility of women through forced sterilization, intimidation, manipulation through propaganda and the legal denial of medical aid. Governments often only receive development aid if they agree to pursue an active population policy. Western drug companies and politicians both have an interest in reducing the birth rate in the Third World. It is not so much a matter of controlling population growth as controlling the population itself. This becomes more urgent as oppositions and tensions grow and unemployment and urbanization assume unmanageable proportions.

Population policy is directed mainly at poor women and is often no more than a euphemism for deliberate selective population growth. In the Philippines, women have no right to medical assistance and housing. Multinationals such as General Motors, Universal Oil Products and the Chase Manhattan Bank, which finance humanitarian organizations involved in birth control, and western leaders who state that 'five dollars invested in population control has more effect than a hundred dollars invested in economic growth' (Lyndon Johnson) are not interested in solving the economic problems of ethnic minorities and the weak sections of the population. The right to birth control means nothing as long as the conditions under which children are born and grow up do not alter. Those who have interests in birth control often use the argument that it is a step toward the emancipation of women when selling their policies in the Third World. Western feminists have not always recognized the dangers attached to campaigns for birth control. The resistance to population policy by Third World women is often directed against potential allies: 'despite such a direct attack on women's rights, population control has been blamed on feminism. This is a most painful irony for feminists.'[17]

History shows that the ideal of motherhood is restored to honour when it is politically and economically opportune; when there is a need for healthy soldiers or when the need for female labour diminishes. Anna Davin has studied imperialist and military motives behind the encouragement of women to become better mothers in England at the turn of the century.[18] Fascist regimes have also glorified motherhood in an extreme way. Throughout European history women have been urged at various times to bear children as a duty to race and nation. In the Third World, propaganda also reminds women of their 'duty as mothers'. There it means that women must have fewer children. In addition to propaganda and financial incentives, coercion, manipulation, inserting the coil without consultation and sterilization without consultation are also used. Women have been used as guinea pigs in research. The pill was first tried out on Bolivian women.

Legal abortion as a free choice is also an essential part of any contraception programme, in Latin America and other Third World countries. Our western struggle for free abortion and a safe means of controlling how many children we have and the Third World struggle against population policy are one and the same. This struggle to control our own bodies is obscured by divisive propaganda.

Development aid, a term still used, is one component in the struggle for political and economic independence in the Third World. Mostly it is a mere palliative, a temporary relief that perpetuates underdevelopment and unequal relations. After the Second World War the dominant thinking behind development aid was that foreign capital to poor countries could help economic progress and eventually enable them to catch up with the wealthy countries. Development aid became a legitimate way for western governments to pursue their economic interests, in particular when the black continent began to 'ferment'. Optimism ceased when the aid-giving countries discovered that poor countries went bankrupt because of balance of payments problems and became poorer while the rich got richer. Economic growth and increased productivity, a more equal distribution of wealth and support for self-determination became the goals of development policy. It became obvious that the difference was not between rich and poor countries, but between a small rich elite and a poor exploited population, an 'underdevelopment' which also occurs in prosperous countries.

Recent years saw a new phase in development relations. An industrialization drive has been set in motion on a wide scale in the Third World. This was not a result of western development policy or of a higher standard of development in developing countries, but rather because new technologies in transport, communication and organization make control over production by industrial companies less dependent on geographical distances. 'International division of labour' and 'new economic order' have become catchwords in development thinking. In the view of development economists like Jan Tinbergen, developing countries must set up labour intensive industries and industrialized countries must concentrate on capital intensive production. The thinking behind this view is that industrialization creates employment, education opportunities, technological development and thus leads to an improvement in standards of living. Exported industrialization does not, however, contribute any of these.[19]

A number of labour intensive industries have been transferred to 'low-wage' countries. These include textile and food industries and also fine electronics. As a result more and more women are losing their jobs in the west. It is mainly women who are employed in the new industries in North Africa and Southeast Asia. Their jobs require no further qualification than their nimble fingers. They work under unhealthy and unsafe labour conditions, do dirty work, are badly paid and often sexually exploited. The pattern of paid work for women often disrupts traditional family patterns and threatens their chance of marriage in countries where wage labour for women is not considered a respectable activity. Where men are the traditional heads of family, whole communities are disrupted when daughters of seventeen suddenly become breadwinners.

The result of this international division of labour is that women in the west lose their jobs, industrialization in the Third World creates more work opportunities for men – women are again the first to be sacked when newer technology is introduced – and women as producers are pushed into the background because the work they have done for centuries is taken away.

Development policy oriented towards improvements in farming methods does not benefit women. The Green Revolution for example has dramatically altered the way women work in agriculture. Mechanization has excluded women in Southeast Asia from the rice harvest. The introduction of cash wages – to men – instead of payment in kind (rice) has made women dependent on the decisions of their husbands.

Development workers and bureaucrats are still talking about the small farmer whose position has to be improved. For African women nothing remains but to run around giggling as development workers explain new techniques to their husbands, that they will have to implement.

Development plans do not work out, so an awareness is slowly growing that women cannot escape the existing division of labour. The economic growth figures do not reflect any increase in economic activity, as gradually, industrialization and mechanization displace subsistence activities with work yielding a wage or income. If unpaid women's work in the harvest is replaced by paid male labour, this does not mean that productivity increases, although it does lead to a rising national income. At policy level people are gradually realizing the contribution women make to the development process. In International Women's Year (1975) it was discovered that development programmes are not specifically directed to women's needs. Most emancipation projects which resulted from this, however, still use stereotypes of the relationship between women and men. Projects aimed at the alleviation of women's work in the home fail to understand that that is not enough. Less to do means a loss of status for women. Suggestions are needed about how women can achieve an independent position. The women's project that began in the Netherlands after 1975, an expensive show-piece for ex-minister Pronk, the Women and Development project in Leiden, is isolated, both from development policy and from the women's movement. A women's farm was set up in Sri Lanka, but this can achieve little if a number of essential questions are not asked about the perspective of the women's cooperative and whether existing power relations are challenged, or how women from different classes can achieve solidarity through cooperation. For the poorest women such a farm becomes a means for survival rather than a liberation.[20] The greatest fear of the researchers is that the farm could fail because of rivalry between women.

It is important, when setting up women's projects, to support the initiatives of women themselves. We would like to go through a number of points again and examine their importance to us as women in the industrialized world.

Imperialism in the Third World plunders women, their energy, their bodies and their children. The work and fertility of women are manipulated according to the needs of centres of power. Sexual imperialism forces women in the Third World into the margins of society. Western women are played off against them: our demands for good contraception are imposed on them and are used to force them into the western family model They are played off against us, we are urged to give up jobs in textiles, and provide work opportunities to women far away.

Everywhere in the world women's work fulfils a specialized 'buffer' function, but there are clear differences between industrialized countries and the Third World:

(1) The buffer function of women in the Third World goes beyond their own economy, which is not oriented to the domestic market. It helps to maintain the gap between underdevelopment in their own countries and prosperity in the industrialized countries.

(2) Third World women are responsible for certain areas of care and upbringing that in highly capitalist countries are socialized and institutionalized into collective and state provision, such as care for the elderly, assistance in childbirth and childcare. This care is not paid for. Migration and urbanization have caused the breakdown of traditional roles without presenting alternatives.

(3) The household economy, a remnant of the original mode of production, is independent of the man's wages. Women's work in the Third World therefore defines the level of poverty in the community. It is the difference between living and surviving. Women are directly confronted with poverty and feel necessities more clearly. Housework comprises many more activities, requires

more skills, such as bread-baking and food-processing, than in industrialized countries. Merely advocating an alleviation of tasks makes little sense if this is not complemented with possibilities of learning new skills for new roles.

There are other differences between the position of women in the Third World and in the West. Family relations still determine a great part of social life, material production and cultural traditions, such as giving in marriage and clitoridectomy. In situations of political and economic insecurity women are often heads of the family and heterosexual relationships are not stable. Family relationships often cannot be compared to the western family pattern at all.

In looking for similar experiences we must avoid the trap of making a simplistic comparison with our own past history. Third World women are not running a hundred years behind. Their position is not comparable with that of women at the dawn of the industrial revolution in Europe, as is often thought, nor will their countries go through the same process as industrialized countries have done. Unilinear thinking denies that Europe and the United States have created underdeveloped countries. Accelerated industrialization, within the context of dependence, is no solution but simply increases the inequality and poverty if profits go to re-investment, speculation and military expenditure. Companies transfer production to those countries because women keep labour costs low. In this context population policies that take away women's reproductive freedom are no remedy for poverty. History demonstrates that the number of children decreases only after prosperity increases.

We must support the political struggles of different peoples and in particular of women for self-determination. The resistance of Third World women to political repression is growing. The question of which women you are in solidarity with and how best to organize international support is dealt with next.

There has been resistance to imperialist oppression in many Third World countries. In countries like Angola, Mozambique, Guinea Bissau, Vietnam and Cuba the struggle for national independence has been successful, often after many years. The nucleus of that resistance was the liberation movements. After independence these became communist parties.

Other forms of resistance to the domination and political power of western countries also exist. Populist national fronts, directed against internal repression, have developed in Iran and Nicaragua. In Nicaragua the Sandinista movement succeeded in uniting the opposition against the dictator Somoza. In the Palestine Liberation Organization (PLO) the accent is on a recognition of the right of Palestinians to their own nation rather than on the development of a socialist society in Palestine. Liberation movements therefore need not result in socialism. The movements described below often began with the fight against colonialism and for national independence and only gradually developed a vision of a socialist society as an answer to oppression, imperialism and capitalism. These movements did not stop at political independence, but strove for a society of 'new', aware people. Women made their own contribution to this, a contribution coloured by their history and traditions.

Left wing liberation movements view the liberation of women as integral to the construction of a new society and provide conditions for women's resistance to be organized. Although they are not primarily concerned with women's questions themselves, the leaders of the liberation movements nevertheless realize that liberation struggles need the women's support. There are many well known quotations from leaders of liberation movements in which a link is made between women's oppression and imperialism. Mao Tse-Tung used the image of four thick ropes which constricted the Chinese woman: politics, the clan, religion and men. These ropes could only be broken by a communist revolution. Ho Chi Minh, the Vietnamese leader, said: 'Women form half of society. If women are not free then society can never be free.' In Oman, the liberation movement (PFLO) passed a resolution in 1968: 'A socialist who is not a feminist cannot call himself a good socialist.' In the Portuguese ex-colonies and in Cuba leaders have made similar statements.

All liberation movements explicitly link women's oppression and imperialism. They also acknowledge that women are doubly oppressed, not only by social structures, but also by men. In Guninea Bissau the liberation organization (PAIGC)[21] used the image of two colonialisms, that of the Portuguese and that of the men, to illustrate this.

Women's issues receive much attention in speeches and posters, but these must be viewed from both sides. The fight against imperialism is the most important and it is within this context that liberation movements analyze the struggle against women's oppression. It is continually stressed that women's liberation can only be realized in a socialist society and that women must fight for socialism.

The attention given to women's liberation is not just the result of the goodwill and revolutionary vision of leaders. Women organized independently to achieve it. Indeed they have been doing so for some time with or without the approval of men. In Cuba and Mozambique women formed their own division within the liberation army. This was viewed by men with a mixture of admiration, confusion and fear. Often women help the army with food, uniforms and information. In the villages, in the liberated regions of former colonies, women do not wait until their participation or contribution is asked for. They demand their own share in the village councils and in the construction of the economy.

The support of women is indispensable to guerrillas. Guerrilla warfare can only succeed if there are power bases in the rural areas and if the population supports the fighters (female and male) with food, shelter and information. The active involvement of the local population is a condition for success. In the villages it is often women who supply food. In Mozambique women carry out 70 per cent of the work in the villages and in Zimbabwe women form up to 95 per cent of the adult population in rural areas. Without them no battle can be won. Women play a key role in the resistance. Time and again they have proved more militant, more courageous and more persevering than men.

The action of women who step out of their traditonal restricted role makes unity of the population possible and strengthens the struggle. Accordingly, counteractivities of occupying armies are often aimed directly at women. The growing self-awareness of women and their efforts has won revolutionary leaders over to women's liberation. Women's liberation is a bitter necessity, for the women themselves and for the successful reconstruction of their country. Samora Machel, now president of Mozambique, rightly states that women's liberation was not a question of charity.[22]

Women struggle in different ways. Their situation partially restricts them because they are often tied to children and home, but this also enables them to undertake activities which are impossible for men. They seem innocent and can exploit this. Women of the Namibian liberation movement (SWAPO) function as couriers and spies, because it is easier for them to obtain travel documents and passes. They smuggle rifles, camouflaged under babyclothes. Dutch women also used this method during the Second World War. In Algeria during the war of independence women hid ammunition and grenades under their wide Arab garments. French soldiers could not search the veiled women for fear of violating sexual and religious codes.

The longer the conflict lasts, the more likely women are to demand a share in military activity. We mentioned the women's divisions in Cuba and Mozambique. In Nicaragua in 1978 women played a top level role in the Sandinista liberation front. Dora Maria Tellez was one of the three commanders in the presidential palace siege. The influence of women on political and military decision making is not, however, always clear from eyewitness reports and the literature.

After the revolution women become involved in the construction of a new society. It is important that they agree on how to make women's problems visible, and find organizations for supporting one another as the struggle continues. They must be aggressive in order to learn how to live together. They need political support in their own country, but feminism in the west can also be a source of power, as Martha Ford, secretary of the SWAPO women's association has said.[23]

In China the 'speak out bitterness' groups, set up after the revolution, encouraged women to fight their oppression. In Cuba courses in sewing and childcare encouraged women to meet and talk outside the home. Practical activities must be accompanied by political education which relates to women's experiences. Women in China learned how to handle tractors and ploughs which until then had been taboo for them. In Mozambique education goes together with health instruction and practical activities such as digging latrines. Political education is important in teaching women how to stick up for their own rights in spite of opposition and how to take part in political decision making. Otherwise women become vulnerable to slogans such as 'what the revolution needs is more babies'.

Women take part in district and village councils. Here they are responsible for tasks which have always been done by women, especially food provision, which has now become part of collective decision making. The collectivization gives the work a political character and as a result women demand the right to decision making in more areas. In Guinea Bissau, for example, the female members of the elected village councils were specially entrusted with the provision of rice for the guerrilla army. But the admission to higher levels of decision making generally comes slowly. Party leaders are still male.

In the struggle men begin to see women as comrades. The fact that women are working without the protection of institutions such as marriage and the traditional family makes this easier. If the army is dependent on women and if women everywhere are breaking out of stereotypes by handling weapons at least as well as men, this forces the men to think about equality. They finally see women as people. In addition to respect, however, they also feel fear and envy, and may consciously exclude women from armed struggle. That happened in Guinea Bissau. As a consolation it was said that all work for the revolution is equally important. But power and weapons go hand in hand.

Even if the resistance of women is recognized, as in the struggle against the enforced removal to reservations in Mozambique, against the homelands policy in South Africa, against political repression and torture, and if the importanc of women's liberation is confirmed within the liberation movement, women still have obstacles to overcome. These are not specific to liberation movements in the Third World, they are the well known reactions of men all over the world. Attempts to isolate the women's struggle by making women's demands ridiculous, by declaring women's demands to be divisive for class unity, are familiar. Feminism can become a term of abuse, good for a club of western oriented women, who have nothing else to do.[24] This is made worse because women in the Third World experience their struggle not as a specifically feminist one.

The lack of education among women hinders the formation of a well trained cadre for women's organizations. During the liberation struggle this cadre of the women's section consisting mainly of women who have had a little more education than the average woman, is often stationed abroad. After liberation the women's organization runs the risk of isolation and of not uniting in the interests of most women. In Mozambique this danger slowed down the growth of women's organization. Women's collective ideas and organization need time to develop. In some districts and villages informal meetings are organized at which men are invited to speak about the problems women have to face. The discussions are often lively. The authority of men is discussed, as well as the attitudes of women. Patriarchy, however, is never mentioned, and these discussions deny any idea of a battle between the sexes as a perspective on women's struggle. Fidel Castro, whose ideas on the Cuban revolution granted an important theoretical place to women's liberation, had to admit retrospectively that in the beginning he unwittingly understimated the resistance and courage of women.

After liberation, various processes can undermine the women's struggle. A stream always develops in emancipation movements which harks back to the old culture. The search for one's own culture and traditions can be a unifying force and therefore liberation movements encourage such searches. But it can turn into conservatism and into reaching for strongly patriarchal expressions of 'culture' such as clitoridectomy, or revival of the veil, as happened in Islamic cultures in Algeria and Iran.

Immediately after liberation the longing for a normal, peaceful life is great, among war veterans in particular. This can exert enormous pressure on women to go back to the home and children. In Cuba women had to fight actively against this. After a war the whole society is in a crisis situation. Trade relations are broken off or boycotted (Mozambique in relation to Rhodesia and the United States in relation to Cuba), which means a loss in foreign exchange. Families are broken up, social structures are destroyed and there is an exodus of the old colonial experts while new experts and technicians are scarcely to be found. This turbulent period creates a need for a stable social focus and the family can provide it. So new socialist countries may place an emphasis on monogamous marriage and a comradely family life. This can mean a new oppression for women, who were active in the liberation struggle and are now required to give up their independence.[25] Afterwards it may take a long time before oppression is identified with the family. Monogamy can be an answer to oppressive practices such as polygamy, marrying off (Mozambique) and double sexual standards (Cuba). It can be seen as an advance as well as a step back. It may also be years before such progress becomes reality for women in remote rural areas.

Prostitution developed and became an enormous social problem under colonialism. New socialist countries therefore find themselves forced to tackle the problem of prostitutes. Unfortunately this often goes together with a condemnation of non-heterosexual relations. This may appear to be a crude repression of sexual freedom or puritanism. But in recent years there has been a relaxation in the assessment of non-heterosexual relations, as in Cuba.

The liberation war provides women with the opportunity to develop their talents both at the front and in health care, education and food provision. Organization is necessary to reach more women. The setting up of a separate women's organization, something which has been done in all new socialist countries shortly before or after independence, is often preceded by intense discussion. Discussions centre on whether priority should be given to the class struggle over the women's struggle and whether a separate organization for women is necessary. These questions are put both by male revolutionaries and by existing women's groups and organizations. Sometimes a women's organization starts as a merger of existing women's groups, as in Cuba. In other countries it emerges from the women's section of the liberation movement, as in Angola and Mozambique.

The creation of women's organizations is not usually the result of massive women's activity. Most organizations begin with a limited cadre which has to make an enormous effort to expand into an organization that can represent the interests of women in the country. They organize women in practical, often traditional female occupations, which are part of the daily routine: childcare, first aid, sewing courses, hygiene and antenatal care. Practical courses are combined with political education. In this way women learn the role they can occupy in the new society, and at the same time what barriers they have to overcome to achieve equality with men. The women's organization also encourages women to take an active part in public discussions and in the construction of people's democracy. It also supports women candidates for people's councils. The women's organization is not always open to all women. Sometimes a potential member may have to prove that she wants to be active.

Women's organizations in the new socialist countries have a dual aim: to support, stimulate and organize women at all social levels and to express women's demands within society as a whole. They also attempt to draw women into the general work outlined by the communist party. When they have gained experience in the second area, they move toward work in the first area, as happened in the movement in Mozambique (OMM).[26]

In most women's organizations the ideas on women's oppression remain in the socialist tradition. Emancipation is not seen separately from the struggle against capitalism, imperialism and oppressive cultural traditions. Although experiences from eastern Europe have shown that 'equality with men' and 'work outside the home' are no guarantees for the creation of a 'new woman', this remains the main perspective of women's organizations. Patriarchy as system of oppression scarcely figures in the analysis. When a man reacts to his wife's attempts to emancipate herself, he is called 'backward' or 'afraid' and has to be re-educated. Most organizations are involved in consciousness-raising, especially among women who have found it difficult to adjust. They stress that no woman is too old to change and to learn.

Women's organizations tackle various problems. Just like other mass organizations for youth, peasants and trade unionists, they have limited autonomy. Their structures can be compared with women's groups in the west who are linked to political parties.

They exert pressure at policy level, but they cannot act in opposition to the party or hold feminist ideas which are hostile to the party. So, although they are familiar with discussions in the feminist movement, they do not identify with them, for fear of a well-meant, renewed colonialism.

Often a women's organization collaborates closely with ministries on advisory bodies for projects aimed at women. The Cuban women's organization (FMC)[27] played an important role in the drafting of Cuban family law. Considerable tensions arise from this partial dependence. Many women would prefer a less defensive attitude.

Also difficult is the relation between the various groups of women that make up the women's organization. Peasants, city dwellers, young and old, housewives and women working outside the home all make their own demands. To organize all women, you have to take differences in life styles and interests into account. Women students turn away because they find little for them. Full time housewives who do most of the organizing work resent the favourable treatment given to women who work outside the home, who use the (still scarce) crèches. In Mozambique rural and urban women within the women's organization (OMM) do not get on. The organizations try to develop a policy for each group, not always successfully.

If the young socialist state is confronted with famine, illiteracy and political and economic isolation in the critical first years after the revolution, there are problems. The women's organizations usually have political support. Committed activists initiate the work, and become the backbone of the organization. Lack of training and organizational experience, transport and communications problems are drawbacks, and women often have to fight men, who treaten to throw them out of the house if they become members.

It remains to assess to what extent and when, a national women's organization is progressive and to what degree it might hold back women's liberation.

'The revolution within the revolution' offers hope for women in Third World countries, but also raises questions. Until now liberation movements have offered Third World women their opportunity to fight for freedom, just as liberation movements have been the only hope for independence. The social differences between women in the Third World and between those women and women in the west are great. These differences determine how women can support one another: from moral support among female political prisoners to organized forms of solidarity aimed at making women's problems visible and known to the world. The existence of a separate women's section in liberation movements is a recognition that women have extra obstacles to overcome. The separate organization of women does not, however, necessarily lead to awareness and a liberated outlook. If women collaborate with one another in a severely separated women's world, as in Islamic cultures, this can increase their oppression and consolidate class privileges. Collaboration does not necessarily lead to solidarity, however; women can also strengthen their oppression and consolidate class privileges.[28]

Solidarity is not a term we can use just as we like. It reflects social relationships between women as well as differences in how we experience our womanhood. Solidarity is not only sympathy and commitment, but also criticism and making demands on one another. The political and material support of western left wing groups and feminists is indispensable for Third World women. For our part we can learn from their perseverance and fighting spirit as well as their achievements in overcoming the traditional division of labour.

Imperialism uses women's isolation to disrupt possible solidarity. We have to fight our traditional roles and not be so eager to believe we cannot support liberation struggles unless they are an obvious attack on 'machismo' and sexual violence. On the other hand, we must not disregard differences and forget about our own interests. We have to examine the economic, cultural and political backgrounds that lead to different perceptions of motherhood, of the right to waged labour. We do have interests in common, despite the contradictions. In recent years various forms of solidarity have developed in the women's movement in the Netherlands. Solidarity action, such as the collection of bras and sanitary towels for fighting women in Namibia is one. We have also set up our own communications and information network, (ISIS Bulletin and

'Domitila' international women's solidarity action group). Publicity is important in disseminating knowledge about women's struggle in the Third World.[29]

We strengthened our presence in existing women's groups (in NCO and NOVIB) in order to exert influence on development policy.[30] Or we formed critical groups within anti-imperialist groups and solidarity committees. Women's groups have emerged alongside women's sections within liberation movements in many solidarity committees. These organize support for campaigns, make their own contacts and prepare their own agitational material. They exist in the Dutch Anti-Apartheid Movement (AABN), Venceremos, the Palestine committee and the Indonesia committee. They experience many problems and have to fight for the right to decide on the scope of their work. The Third World movement paid little attention to the position of women and why women join the liberation struggle and what happens to them after independence. The liberation movements don't realise that they cannot make endless demands on the energy of women volunteers here, if they do not, at the same time, want to recognize the specific interests of those volunteers. This becomes more impossible where male volunteers occupy staff positions and female volunteers do all the practical work.

We do not need to physically cross national boundries for our solidarity work. The Moroccan women's committee, the Bolivian women's group, the Union of Turkish women and the Foreign Women's Consultative Group are all female political refugees or foreign women in the Netherlands. We can work with them here. We are enthusiastic about what women can do in new socialist countries and we can learn from them. Until now human relations have not been regarded as political. Many problems have not been analyzed, such as the influence of the heterosexual norm on relations between women and men.

The gap cannot be bridged easily. It is difficult for us to understand women with a different history and a different culture. We must learn to think differently in order to understand their situation. Even if we get angry when we recognize our own problems in their situation, many questions still remain. The exchange of experiences is the backbone of our solidarity. Women cannot wait until after the revolution.

Notes

1. The women's movement and motherhood

We should like to thank Annemiek Hoogenboom, Marga Ouwehand and Ingrid Vorrink for a critical reading of the draft of this chapter.
1. Here we are following Ann Oakley's description of 'motherhood ideology': 1) all women must become mothers (because of their 'nature' the only possible 'gratification of appetite'); 2) all mothers need their children; 3) all children need their mother. Ann Oakley, *Woman's Work. The Housewife, Past and Present*, New York: Vintage Books, 1976, p. 186; European edition: *Housewife*, London: Penguin, 1974.
2. In addition to the books and journals specifically mentioned we have also used: Marjo van Soest, Eva Besnyö, Hennie van der Zande, *Meid, wat ben ik bewust geworden. Vijf jaar Dolle Mina*, The Hague: Stichting Uitgeverij Dolle Mina, 1975; Dymphie van Berkel, *et al.*, *Moederschap is mijn achilleshiel. Een boek over kracht en kwetsbaarheid*, Zeist: Uitgeverij Stichting Trezoor, 1979; data from the doctoral research group Motherhood, Department of Women's Studies, Faculty of Social Sciences, University of Amsterdam (research report in preparation); in particular: Diet Scholten, and Joke Grosz, 'Verslag van een onderzoek naar moederschap en tweede feministiese golf'; Boston Women's Health Book Collective, *Ourselves and Our Children*, New York: Random House, 1978.
3. The interview with Simone de Beauvoir appeared in *Opzij*, feminist monthly, October 1977.
4. De Bonte Was, *Moederboek*, Amsterdam: Feministische

Uitgeverij de Bonte Was, 1976.

5. Shulamith Firestone, *The Dialectic of Sex*, New York: William Morrow, 1970.

6. For a critique of these ideas of Firestone, see: Juliet Mitchell, *Woman's Estate*, London: Penguin, 1971, pp. 87–91 and Zillah Eisenstein, 'Developing a theory of capitalist patriarchy' in Zillah Eisenstein, (ed.), *Capitalist Patriarchy and the Case for Socialist Feminism*, New York and London: Monthly Review Press, 1979, pp. 5–41.

7. As analysis of women's oppression this view is put forward by a large part of Dolle Mina. For Man-Woman-Society (MVM) and the 'discussion group movement' this was not so clearly the case. But in MVM and in Dolle Mina the emphasis lay on removing obstacles to enable women to go out to work. The 'discussion group movement' did not demand and act publicly, as did other clubs.

8. That a problem of choice exists is of course closely connected to the increased use of contraceptives, which makes a certain degree of planning possible. If children can be planned it seems to be the individual woman's choice.

9. See for example Linda Gordon, 'De strijd voor vrijheid van reproduktie: drie stadia in het feminisme' in *Socialisties-Feministiese Teksten* 3, 1979, p. 55.

10. Sheila Kitzinger, *Women as Mothers*, London: Fontana, 1978, p. 29.

11. For more comment on the problem of choice see: Lidy Beukers, and Geraldine Blokland, 'Moederschap, keuze of lot' in *Moeder word je niet vanzelf*, a collection of articles on motherhood, Amsterdam: Pedagogies-Didakties Instituut van de Universiteit van Amsterdam, 1979.

12. *Vrouwenkrant Amsterdam*, March 1973, p. 19; quoted by Scholten and Grosz, *op. cit*.

13. Monika Jaeckel, and Greta Tüllmann, 'Die aktuelle Gretchenfrage heisst: 'Wie stehst du zur Mütterfrage in *Frauen und Mütter*, Berlin: Verein 3. Sommeruniversität für Frauen, 1978, 1979.

14. See also: Corinne de Beer, 'Patriarchaat en kindervijandigheid' in *Moeder word je niet vanzelf*, pp. 87–97.

15. See for a corresponding critique the article by Joyce Outshoorn

elsewhere in this volume.

16. Anja Meulenbelt, 'Over politiek bewustzijn en de kwestie met de "mannelijkheid"' in *Socialisties-Feministiese Teksten* 1, 1978, pp. 94–124.

17. A group of women in the Women's Studies Department in the Faculty of Social Sciences of the University of Amsterdam has studied the subject of Collectivization of domestic work. For an interim report see: Saskia Poldervaart, 'Kollektivering van huishoudelijke arbeid' in *Wetenschap en Samenleving*, June/July 1979, pp. 48–58.

18. This subject is also under discussion in the West German women's movement. See Siebenschön, 'Plädoyer zur Abschaffung der Väter', a series of three articles in *Emma, Zeitschrift für Frauen von Frauen*, Cologne, Jan., Feb., March 1979.

19. Adrienne Rich in *Of Woman Born, Motherhood as Experience and Institution*, New York: Norton, 1976.

20. Marianne Braun, 'Het personen- en familierecht, de wet-geschiedenis van de maritale macht in een notedop'. Unpublished paper, University of Amsterdam (Institute for Political Science), 1980.

21. A comparable problem is the question of the 'legitimacy' of children in England at present; see Natasha Spedding, 'How dare you presume I'm legitimate' in *Spare Rib*, No 85, August 1979, p. 46.

22. Barbara Ehrenreich and Deirdre English describe how in the 1950s in the United States this father-role was gradually made into a norm by psychologists and pedagogues. They connect up the 'need' for identification with fathers with the moral slackness of American soldiers which emerged in the Korean war and they illustrate how the so called 'indulgent mother' got the blame for this slackness. Barbara Ehrenreich and Deirdre English, *For Her Own Good*, New York: Anchor Press/Doubleday, and London: Pluto 1978.

23. Barbara Seaman, 'The Dangers of oral contraception' in Claudia Dreifus (ed.), *Seizing Our Bodies*, New York: Vintage Books, 1978.

24. The question is whether women want to fuck so eagerly, so much and so often that they are prepared to suffer daily hormone

intakes particulary now that many more women are aware that the vaginal orgasm is a myth. The pill is still so popular probably because swallowing a pill is much easier than wearisome resistance to male definitions of sexuality.

25. Linda Gordon, *Woman's Body, Woman's Right. A Social History of Birth Control in America*, London: Penguin, 1977, p. xiii.

26. See also Joyce Outshoorn's chapter elsewhere in this volume.

27. The only exception to the marxist idea that the decisive moment in history is the mode of production, is the remark by Friedrich Engels that reproductive relations are also decisive. See *inter alia* Joyce Outshoorn's chapter elsewhere in this volume.

28. Gayle Rubin, 'The traffic in women. Notes on the "political economy" of sex', in Rayna R. Reiter (ed.), *'Toward an Anthropology of Women'*, New York and London: Monthly Review Press 1975.

29. Nancy Chodorow, *The Reproduction of Mothering. Psychoanalysis and the Sociology of Gender*, Berkeley, Los Angeles and London: University of California Press, 1978; see also Aafke Komter elsewhere in this volume.

30. A survey of various traditional methods of birth control can be found *inter alia* in: Gordon, *op. cit.*

31. cf. *inter alia* Jan de Bruin, *Geschiedenis van de abortus in Nederland. Een analyse van opvattingen en discussies 1600*-1979, Amsterdam: Van Gennep, 1979, pp. 63-121.

32. Ann Oakley, 'Wisewoman and Medicine man: changes in the management of childbirth' in Juliet Mitchell, and Ann Oakley (eds.), *The Rights and Wrongs of Women*, London: Penguin, 1976; Barbara Ehrenreich, and Deirdre English, *Witches, Midwives and Nurses. A History of Woman Healers*, London: Compendium, 1974.

33. See Ria van Hengel, 'Het heroveren van de geboorte' in *Lover*, quarterly literary survey for the women's movement, 1978, III, pp. 103-6.

34. See for an example of such a reaction Emma Brunt and Lodewijk Brunt, 'Zedelijk leven. Op zoek naar het begin' in *De Gids*, No 9/10, 1979.

35. On the glorifying of the mother-role to raise a low birth rate see for example: Anet Bleich and Mieke Aerts, 'Vrouwen en fascisme' in *Socialisties-Feministiese Teksten* 1, 1978, pp. 239-63. The

relation between population policy and British imperialism around the turn of the century is well described by Anna Davin, 'Imperialism and motherhood' in *History Workshop*, 5, Spring 1978, pp. 9–69.

36. See for example Annemiek Hoogenboom, and Annemieke Voets, elsewhere in this volume and Gordon, *op. cit.*, ch. 13: 'A Note on Population control.'

37. Rich, in *Of Woman Born.*, p. 317.

2. Domestic and public

1. Research by Yvonne van der Doelen for A. de Swaan, 'Uitgaans-beperking en uitgaansangst: over de verschuiving van bevelshuishouding naar onderhandelingshuishouding' in *De Gids*, 8/1979, p. 486.

2. See, for example, W.H. Posthumus-van der Goot, *et al.*, *Van Moeder op Dochter: de Maatschappelijke Positie van de Vrouw in Nederland vanaf de Franse Tijd*, Nijmegen: SUN-reprint, 1977, p. 44.

3. Dr Aletta M. Jacobs, *Herinneringen*, Nijmegen: SUN-reprint, 1978, pp. 70–2.

4. Yolanda and Robert Murphy, *Women of the Forest*, New York: Columbia University Press, 1974, pp. 109, 137.

5. Tennyson, *The Princess*. Quoted by Catherine Hall, 'De geschiedenis van de huisvrouw' in *Te Elfder Ure, Feminisme I*, 1975, p. 695.

6. Eli Zaretsky, *Capitalism, the Family and Personal Life*, London: Pluto Press, 1976.

7. *Meid, wat ben ik bewust geworden: 5 jaar Dolle Mina*, The Hague: Stichting Uitgeverij Dolle Mina, 1975, pp. 7 ff.

8. An arbitrary collection of studies: Catherine Hall, *op. cit.* (plus the supplement on the Netherlands by Selma Leijdesdorff). Patricia Branca, *Silent Sisterhood: Middle-Class Women in the Victorian Home*, London: Croom Helm, 1975. Nancy Cott, *The Bonds of Womanhood: 'Woman's Sphere' in New England, 1780–1835*, New Haven: Yale University Press, 1977. Carroll Smith-Rosenberg, *et al.*, 'The Female World of Love and Ritual: Relations between women in nineteenth-century America' in *Signs*, I, 1,

1975. Werkgroep Vrouwengeschiedenis Groningen, *Vrouwen, Kiesrecht en Arbeid: Nederland 1889–1919*, Groningen, 1977. Selma Leijdesdorff, *Verborgen Arbeid, Vergeten Arbeid*, Assen: Van Gorcum, 1977.

9. Whom I reckon to belong to the women's movement without further discussion.

10. This chapter is not a 'history' of the Women's Anthropology Group of Amsterdam.

11. This group published a book on the occasion of the International Woman's Year 1975: Els Postel-Koster, and Joke Schrijvers, *Vrouwen op Weg*, Assen: Van Gorcum, 1976.

12. The first publication of the Women's Anthropology Group appeared in 1977: *'Vrouw in Zicht!' Naar een feministiese antropologie*, 3rd edn., Amsterdam: SUA, 1979. I only joined the group at the end of 1977.

13. Michelle Rosaldo, and Louise Lamphere (eds.), *Woman, Culture and Society*, Stanford: Stanford University Press, 1974.

14. *ibid.*, pp. 17–42.

15. The English terms Michelle Rosaldo uses are domestic and public.

16. *ibid.*, p. 24.

17. *ibid.*, pp. 25–35. Michelle Rosaldo also refers to other articles in the same collection, *inter alia* that of Sherry Ortner ('Is female to male as nature is to culture'), Nancy Chodorow ('Family structure and female personality') and Bridget O'Laughlin ('Mediation of contradiction: why Mbum women do not eat chickens').

18. cf. Joyce Outshoorn's remarks on the 'doctrine of forgetfulness' elsewhere in this volume.

19. Robin Fox, *Kinship and Marriage: An Anthropological Perspective*, Harmondsworth: Penguin, 1967.

20. This whole section, including quotations, is based on Fox, *op. cit.*, pp. 31–2.

21. Fox, *op. cit.*, returns only once to the question of whether men always have the power. This is in his examination of the matrilinear kinship system (a system where descent is traced only through the female line). Matrilinear systems were (and are) sometimes mistaken for matriarchal systems; wrongly, as Fox relates. In matrilinear systems men also have more power than

women. He is right in his description, but it is funny how relieved he is that no 'Amazonian' empire has ever been found, where 'men would be of no account and would be used for breeding purposes only.' 'Such a *sinister* practice exists only in the imagination' and 'Women don't ever seem to have got *quite such a grip* on things' (my italics) (Fox, *op. cit.*, p. 113).

22. With respect to 'biology' Fox says that the anthropologist need only concern himself with it in so far as biology places restrictions which no society can evade (*op. cit.*, p. 36).

23. This is also true for left wing anthropologists who are concerned with the connection between primitive modes of production and kinship structures. Cf. the criticisms of Meillassoux, Terray and Godelier in Lucy Bland *et al.*, 'Relations of reproduction: approaches through anthropology' in *Women Take Issue: Aspects of Women's Subordination*, London: Hutchinson, 1978, pp. 155–75.

24. cf. Michelle Rosaldo, 'The use and abuse of anthropology: reflections on feminism and cross-cultural understanding' in *Signs*, V, 3, 1980, pp. 389–417.

25. Well-known reviews which summarize feminist approaches to anthropology are: Louise Lamphere, 'Review Essay: Anthropology' in *Signs*, II, 3, 1977, pp. 612–27. Rayna Reiter, 'Review essay: anthropology' in *Signs*, IV, 3, 1979, pp. 457–513.

26. Ernestine Friedl, 'The position of women' in *Anthropological Quarterly*, XL, 3, 1967; Joyce Riegelhaupt, 'Saloio women: an analysis of informal and formal political and economic roles of Portuguese peasant women' in *Anthropological Quarterly*, XL, 3, 1967; Cynthia Nelson, 'Public and private politics: Women in the Middle Eastern world' in *American Ethnologist*, I, 1974; Susan Carol Rogers, 'Female forms of power and the myth of male dominance: a model of female/male interaction in peasant society' in *American Ethnologist*, II, 1975.

27. Apart from the article in Note 26, Ernestine Friedl also wrote on her field work in *Vasilika: A Village in Modern Greece*, New York: Holt, Rinehart & Winston, 1962.

28. Friedl, '*The position of women*', p. 108.

29. Nelson, *op. cit.*, p. 560.

30. This is not in the article, but is stated in a note in: Susan

Harding, 'Women and words in a Spanish village' in Rayna Rapp Reiter, (ed.), *Toward an Anthropology of Women*, New York and London: Monthly Review Press, 1975, p. 306.
31. That is presumably, why I 'overlooked' two equally relevant articles at the time, by Susan Harding and Rayna Reiter. They were 'too early' with their arguments that women do not have genuine decisive power. Harding, *op. cit.*, and Rayna Rapp Reiter, 'Men and Women in the South of France: public and private domains' in Rayna Rapp Reiter, *Toward an Anthropology*.
32. 'Over politiek bewustzijn and de kwestie met de "manne-lijkheid" in *Socialisties-Feministiese Teksten 1*, 1978, p. 115.
33. New York: Ballantine, 1980, p. 277.
34. Harding, *op. cit.*, p. 308.
35. *ibid.*
36. An extensive discussion of the problems encountered when attempting to distinguish cause and effect is not called for here. I think that the division between public and domestic sphere hampers the liberation of women and 'causes' the maintenance of oppression.
37. See Notes 13 and 14.
38. cf. Selma Sevenhuijsen, 'Vadertje staat, moedertje thuis? Vrouwen, reproductie en de staat' in *Socialisties-Feministiese Teksten* 1, 1978; and Selma Leijdesdorff, *Verborgen Arbeid, Vergeten Arbeid*, Assen: Van Gorcum, 1977, pp. 1–16.
39. De Swaan, *op. cit.*, pp. 490–1.
40. Charlotte Gower Chapman, *Milocca: A Sicilian Village*, London: Allen & Unwin, 1973, Ch. II.
41. Maria Rosa Cutrufelli, *Disoccupata con Onore: Lavoro e Condizione della Donna*, Milan: Mazzotta, 1975, p. 73.
42. Renée Hirschon, 'Open body/closed space: the transformation of female sexuality' in Shirley Ardener, (ed.), *Defining Females: The Nature of Women in Society*, London: Croom Helm, 1978, p. 81.
43. Nelson, *op. cit.*, p. 559.

3. The dual heritage

1. Joan Kelly, 'The doubled vision of feminist theory: a postscript

to the "Women and power" conference', in *Feminist Studies*, 5 1979 1 (Spring), p. 219.

2. Zillah R. Eisenstein, 'Developing a theory of capitalist patriarchy' in Zillah R. Eisenstein (ed.), *Capitalist Patriarchy and the Case for Socialist Feminism*, New York and London: Monthly Review Press, 1979, pp. 16 onwards.

3. Joyce Outshoorn, 'Marx en Engels kijken naar vrouwen' in *Te Elfde Ure 20, 'Feminisme 1*, Nijmegen, SUN 1975 pp. 623–638.

4. F. Engels, *The Origin of the Family, Private Property and the State*, Moscow: Progress Publishers.

5. Kate Millett, *Sexual Politics*, London: Sphere Books, 1971.

6. Shulamith Firestone, *The Dialectic of Sex, The Case for Feminist Revolution*, New York: William Morrow and Company, 1970 (pocket edition, Bantam Books, 1971).

7. Juliet Mitchell, *Women's Estate*, Harmondsworth: Pelican, 1971.

8. *ibid*, p. 99.

9. See e.g. Anja Meulenbelt: 'De ekonomie van de koesterende funktie', in *Te Elfder Ure 20*, *op. cit.*, pp. 638–676; Margaret Benston *et al.*, *De Politieke economie van de huishoudelijke arbeid. Debat over gezin, ekonomie en staat in het huidige kapitalisme*, Nijmegen, SUN, 1977.

10. Maureen Mackintosh, 'Domestic Labour and the Household' in Sandra Burnham (ed.), *Fit Work for Women*, London: Croom Helm, 1979, pp. 174–75. In this article Mackintosh quotes the difference which Mitchell had already made between an economic household and a family. These coincide in western capitalist societies, but Mackintosh shows that e.g. in Senegal these are two different matters.

11. Maxine Molyneux, 'Beyond the domestic labour debate', in *New Left Review* 116, July/August 1979, p. 21.

12. *ibid*., pp. 24–25.

13. Jean Gardiner, Lecture at the Vrije Universiteit, 5 and 6 June, 1980 Amsterdam.

14. Mitchell, *Women's Estate*, pp. 106–107.

15. *ibid*., p. 106.

16. See the article by Selma Sevenhuijsen and Petra de Vries eleswhere in this collection.

17. Russell Jacoby, *Social Amnesia. A Critique of Contemporary Psychology from Adler to Laing*, Boston: Beacon Press, 1975.

18. 'The sign of the times is thought that has succumbed to fashion; it scorns the past as antiquated while touting the present as best', Jacoby, *ibid.*, p. 1.

19. Mary Daly, *Gyn/Ecology. The Metaethics of Radical Feminism*, London: The Womens Press, 1979, p. 348.

20. A few recent Dutch examples: Projektgroep Vormingswerk en Vakbeweging, *Vakbondswerk moet je leren. Leerboek over Industrie-bonden in Engeland, Frankrijk, Duitsland, Nederland, de kaderleden en hun scholing*, Amsterdam: SUA, 1979; Jan Brands et al., *Andere wijs over Onderwijs, Naar een materialistische Onderwijssociologie*, Nijmegen: Link, 1977.

21. Juliet Mitchell, *Psychoanalysis and Feminism*, London: Allen Lane, 1974.
For reviews of this see: Petra de Vries, 'Kanttekeningen bij "De kontroverse over de psychoanalyse in de vrouwenbeweging" ', *Socialisties-Feministiese Teksten, 2*, 1978 p. 198; Veronica Beechey, *op.cit.*, pp. 72–73; Aafke Komter, elsewhere in this volume.

22. See for example: Aafke Komter, essay elsewhere in this collection and: Dalston Study Group 'Was the patriarchy conference patriarchal?', in *Papers on Patriarchy*, Brighton: Women's Publishing Collective, 1976, pp. 76–81.

23. See for example Lucy Bland, Rachel Harrison, Frank Mort and Christine Weedon, 'Relations of production: approaches through anthropology', in *Women Take Issue. Aspects of Women's Subordination*, London: Hutchinson, 1978, p. 161 (Women's Studies Group, Centre for Contemporary Cultural Studies, University of Birmingham).

24. Kate Young and Olivia Harris, 'The subordination of women in cross-cultural perspective' in *Papers on Patriarchy, op. cit.*, pp. 38–53. It is difficult to deduce how much they owe to Gayle Rubin as they only include a list of articles and books without references at the end of that article, in which Rubin is mentioned.

25. Aafke Komter, in *Papers on Patriarchy*.

26. *ibid.* p. 104.

27. Compare the review by Beechey, *op.cit.*, pp. 72 onwards of Mitchell, *Psychoanalysis and Feminism*.

28. See Michele Barrett and Mary McIntosh, 'Christine Delphy, Towards a materialist feminism?' in *Feminist Review*, 1979, no 1, pp. 95–106. Also the review by Beechey of Delphy, *op.cit.*, pp. 70–71.

29. See Nancy Chodorow, *The Reproduction of Mothering, Psychoanalysis and the Sociology of Gender*, Berkeley, Los Angeles and London: University of California Press, 1978.

30. See the article by Saskia Grotenhuis in *Socialisties-Feministies Teksten* 4, 1980.

31. Margaret Mead, *Male and Female: a Study of the Sexes in a Changing World*, New York: Morrow, 1975; Harmondsworth: 1950; and *Sex and Temperament in three Primitive Societies*, New York: Morrow, 1935.

32. There are various collections of anthropological writings which make this clear: Michelle L. Rosaldo and Louise Lamphere (eds.), *Woman, Culture and Society*, Stanford: Stanford University Press, 1974; Rayna Rapp Reiter (ed.), *Towards an Anthropology of Women*, New York and London: Monthly Review Press, 1975; Vrouwengroep antropologie, Vrouw in Zicht, *Naar een feministiese antropologie*, Amsterdam: SUA, 1979; Rayna Rapp Reiter, 'Anthropology Review Essay' in *Signs*, 4, 1979 3, pp. 497–514.

33. Rayna Rapp Reiter, 'Introduction' in Reiter, *op. cit.*, *Towards an Anthropology*, p. 12 (n.b. the writings of this author can be found under the name Reiter as well as the name Rapp).

34. Claude Meillassoux, *Femmes, Greniers et Capitaux*, Paris: Maspero, 1975; B. Hindess and P. Hirst, *Mode of Production and Social Formation*, London: Routledge and Kegan Paul, 1977. For a feminist review of Meillassoux, see: Maureen Mackintosh, 'Reproduction and Patriarchy: a Critique of Meillassoux, *Femmes, Greniers et Capitaux*' in *Capital and Class*, 1, 1977 2, pp. 119–128; and of Hindess and Hirst: Bland *op. cit.*, pp. 156–161.

35. Felicity Edholm, Olivia Harris and Kate Young, 'Conceptualizing Women' in *Critique of Anthropology*, 3, 1977 9/10 Women's Issue), pp. 101–131.

36. This wonderful example is from: Rapp, 'Anthropology', *op. cit.*, p. 508.

37. The term sex-gender system comes from Gayle Rubin.

38. See for example: Joyce Outshoorn, 'Zo vader, zo zoon en van

moeder op dochter' in *Socialisties-Feministiese Teksten 1*, 1977, pp. 67–94.

39. Edholm *et al.*, in 'Conceptualizing women', in *Critique of Anthropology* 3, p. 25

40. Maureen Mackintosh, 'Reproduction and Patriarchy', *op.cit.*

41. *ibid.*, p. 126

42. Rapp, 'Anthropology' in *Signs* 1979 pp. 508–511; Michele Z. Rosaldo, 'Woman, culture and society, A theoretical overview' in Rosaldo and Lamphere (eds.), *op. cit.*, pp. 17–43

43. Gayle Rubin, 'The Traffic in Women', in *Towards an Anthropology of Women*, New York 1975, p. 168

44. *ibid.*, p. 165

45. *ibid.*, p. 163

46. *ibid.*, p. 168

47. *ibid.*, p. 180

48. *ibid.*, p. 180

49. *ibid.*, p. 188

50. *ibid.*, p. 190

51. See the article by Marijke Mossink in *Socialisties Feministiese Teksten 4*, 1980.

52. Edholm *et al.*, 'Conceptualizing women', in *Critique of Anthropology* 3 1977, pp. 120–121

53. Bland *et al.*, in *Women Take Issue – Aspects of Women's Subordination*, op. cit., p. 166.

54. See also: Aafke Komter in '*Papers on Patriarchy*', pp. 115–118

55. *ibid.*, p. 168

56. See particularly the articles by Annette Kuhn and Annmarie Wolpe, 'Feminism and Materialism' in Kuhn and Wolpe, *op.cit.*, pp. 1–11, and Roisin McDonough and Rachel Harrison, 'Patriarchy and the relations of production' in Kuhn and Wolpe, *op.cit.*, pp. 11–42. In the introduction to their collection, Kuhn and Wolpe themselves warn of the dangers of theoreticism (pp. 6–7), but in my eyes some of the articles in this collection do not succeed in avoiding this trap.

57. Kelly, in 'The double vision in feminist theory', *Feminist Studies*, 5, p. 220.

4. Feminism and psychoanalysis

1. J. Lacan, 'La femme n'existe pas', in *Alternative*, Das Lächeln der Medusa. Frauenbewegung, Sprache, Psychoanalyse, June/Aug. 1976, No 108/9.

2. It is interesting to note that Simone de Beauvoir in a recent interview with *Marie-Claire* (June 1978) said that if she had been younger she would again study psychoanalysis but this time from a feminist point of view.

3. I don't claim that this survey is comprehensive, I only try to give a general overview of various writers in the field.

4. See also A. Meulenbelt, 'Over politiek bewustzijn en de kwestie met de "mannelijkheid" ' and S. Sevenhuijsen, 'Vadertje staat moedertje thuis' in *Socialisties-Feministiese Teksten* I, Amsterdam: Feministische Uitgeverij Sara, 1978.

5. For a good survey of the debate in England see: A. Foreman *Femininity as Alienation*, London: Pluto, 1977; in the Netherlands: A. Meulenbelt, 'De ekonomie van de koesterende funktie' in *Te Elfder Ure*, No 20, Feminisme 1, Nijmegen: SUN, 1975 and *Politieke ekonomie van de huishoudelijke arbeid*, Nijmegen: SUN, 1977.

6. D. Dinnerstein, *The Mermaid and the Minotaur*, New York: Harper & Row, 1977, p. 44

7. See S. Freud, 'Einige psychischen Folgen des anatomischen Geschlechtsunterschieds' 1925, *G.W.*, vol. XIV; 'Uber die weibliche Sexualität' 1931, *G.W.*, XIV; 'Die Weiblichkeit' 1932, *G.W.*, vol. XV; *Drei Abhandlungen zur Sexualtheorie*, Fischer, 1976.

8. See also for example S. Burniston, F. Mort, C. Weedon, 'Psychoanalysis and the cultural acquisition of sexuality and subjectivity', in *Women Take Issue, Aspects of Women's Subordination*, London: Hutchinson, 1978.

9. This account is based on J. Lacan, *Ecrits*, Paris: Editions du Seuil, 1966 (here: 'La signification du Phallus'); A. Mooij, *Taal en verlangen, Lacan's theorie van de psychoanalyse*, Meppel: Boom, 1975; *Te Elfder Ure*, Psychoanalyse 1, Nijmegen: SUN, 1976; R. Coward, 'Re-reading Freud, the making of the feminine' in *Spare Rib*, May 1978; Burniston *et al.*, *op. cit.*, Lacan, '*La femme*

n'existe pas'. Lacan's theory is extraordinarily abstract; his language is inaccessible, full of allusions and innuendoes that are unclear immediately to the unsuspecting reader. Lacan's intention is to justify Freud. He does not want to establish any meanings, for terms have no fixed meaning, but borrow their meaning from the context. I have tried to reproduce Lacan's ideas as simply as possible. Freud himself wrote extraordinarily clearly, it seems to me that Lacan's writing is unnecessarily complicated.

10. Lacan, *'La femme n'existe pas'*

11. J. Kristeva, 'Produktivität der Frau', in *Alternative*.

12. J. Kristeva, *Des Chinoises*, Paris: Editions des Femmes, 1974; other publications by Julia Kristeva: *La révolution du langage poétique*, Paris: Editions des Femmes, 1974; *Polylogue*, Paris: Editions du Seuil, 1977.

13. H. Cixous, 'Schreiben, Feminität, Veränderung' in *Alternative*.

14. H. Cixous, C. Clément, 'Die Frau als Herrin?' in *Alternative*; Cathérine Clément appears according to this discussion to believe in the unavoidability of a certain authority in the transfer of knowledge.

15. L. Irigaray, 'Das Geschlecht das nicht Eins ist', in *Ware Körper, Sprache, der verrückte Diskurs der Frauen*, Berlin: Merve Verlag, 1976.

16. L. Irigaray, 'Die Frau, ihr Geschlecht und die Sprache', in *Unbewusstes, Frauen, Psychoanalyse*, Berlin: Merve Verlag, 1977.

17. Irigaray, *Ware, Körper, Sprache*.

18. L. Irigaray, 'Psychoanalyse und weibliche Sexualität: Die Theorie Freuds' and 'Cosi fan tutte', in *Unbewusstes, Frauen, Psychoanalyse*.

19. L. Irigaray, *Spéculum de l'autre femme*, Paris: Editions de Minuit, 1974.

20. M. Plaza, '"Phallomorphic power" and the psychology of "women"', in *Ideology and Consciousness*, No 4, Autumn 1978.

21. L. Irigaray, 'Das Geschlecht das nicht Eins ist', and 'Die Mechanik "des Flüssigen"', in *Unbewusstes, Frauen, Psychoanalyse*.

22. See also L. Irigaray, 'Women's exile', in *Ideology and Consciousness*, No 1, May 1977.

23. J. Lacan, 'Encore', *Séminaire* XX, Paris, 1975 (quoted in Irigaray, 'Così fan tutte').

24. J. Mitchell, *Psychoanalysis and Feminism*, London: Allen Lane, Penguin, 1974.

25. Because in various Dutch publications attention is paid to Juliet Mitchell's thinking (see e.g. *Te Elfder Ure*, No. 20), I do not go into her book in greater detail here.

26. See A. Komter, 'Het "eeuwig" onbewuste', unpublished thesis, Amsterdam, 1975, on Mitchell's book.

27. R. Coward, S. Lipshitz, E. Cowie, 'Psychoanalysis and patriarchal structures', in *Papers on Patriarchy*, London: 1978.

28. What I am doing here is consciously making a complicated text banal; common sense in reading such seemingly interesting arguments shows that when they are 'translated' into ordinary words often very little remains.

29. Dalston Study Group, 'Was the patriarchy conference patriarchal?' in *Papers on Patriarchy*.

30. This discussion is not new: it is a continuation of the so-called Jones-Freud controversy. Jones postulated an individual female sexuality, not derived from the male libido (Karen Horney also subscribed to this idea), while Freud postulated the existence of only one libido, which is male.

31. M. Montrelay, 'Inquiry into femininity', in *M/F*. No 1, 1978.

32. P. Adams, 'Representation and Sexuality', in *M/F*, No 1, 1978.

33. At the moment (February 1979) only two numbers of *M/F* have appeared.

34. S. Lipshitz, 'The personal is political. The problem of feminist therapy', in *M/F*, No 2, 1978; another of Sue Lipshitz's works is *Tearing the Veil. Essays on Femininity*, London: 1978.

35. P. Adams, Jeff Minson, 'The subject of feminism', in *M/F*, No 2, 1978.

36. A. Foreman, *Femininity as Alienation. Women and the Family in Marxism and Psychoanalysis*, London: Pluto, 1977.

37. Ann Foreman uses the terms capitalism and industrialization rather carelessly and interchangeably; see J. Blok, 'Tussen de wal van Marx en het schip van Freud' in *De Groene Amsterdammer*, 24 January 1979.

38. Another German writer who has studied the subject is A. Windhoff-Héritier, *Sind Frauen so wie Freud sie sah?*, Reinbek: Rowohlt, 1976. She offers a strongly sociological re-interpretation of the characteristics of femininity described by Freud, such as narcissism, passivity, masochism, and a weak superego. She does not offer a genuine theory on the emergence of the ideology of the sexes.

39. C. Hagemann-White, 'De kontroverse over de psychoanalyse in de vrouwenbeweging', in *Socialisties-Feministiese Teksten* 2, Amsterdam: Sara, 1978.

40. N. Chodorow, *The Reproduction of Mothering. Psychoanalysis and the Sociology of Gender*, California: University of California Press, 1978.

41. Following Nancy Chodorow I shall henceforth call it 'mothering'.

42. In her article, 'Mothering, Male dominance and capitalism' in Z.R. Eisenstein, (ed.), *Capitalist Patriarchy and the Case for Socialist Feminism*, New York: Monthly Review Press, 1978, Nancy Chodorow further examines the relation between capitalism and the reproduction of certain types of labour force in the family; she also devotes a chapter of the above mentioned book to the subject.

43. See also N. Chodorow, 'Family structure and feminine personality' in M. Rosaldo, L. Lamphere (eds), *Women, Culture and Society*, Stanford: Stanford University Press, 1974.

44. This can lead to 'compulsive masculinity' and hatred of women; see Nancy Chodorow's interesting explanation of this in V. Gornick, B. Moran (eds.), *Women in Sexist Society*, New York: Basic Books, 1971.

45. See Chodorow, *Family Structure and Feminine Personality*.

46. See also J. Baker Miller, in her book *Toward a New Psychology of Women.* She describes the stereotypes that occur in relations between women and men as a result of early childhood experiences.

47. Burniston, Mort and Weedon, '*Psychoanalysis and the cultural acquisition of sexuality and subjectivity*'.

48. A. Rich, *Of Woman Born*, New York: Norton, 1976; Dinnerstein, *The Mermaid and the Minotaur*.

49. Rich, *ibid.*, pp. 212–13.

50. *ibid.*, p. 216.

5. 'The Policing of Families'

1. Elisabeth Wilson, 'Beyond the ghetto: thoughts on "Beyond the Fragments. Feminism and the Making of Socialism" by Hilary Wainwright, Sheila Rowbotham and Lynne Segal' in: *Feminist Review*, 1980, no. 4, p. 40.

2. Jaques Donzelot, *La Police des Familles*, Paris: 1977, with an epilogue by Gilles Deleuze. We refer to the English edition: *The Policing of Families, Welfare vs. the State*, London: 1980. This contains a foreword by Deleuze and by Donzelot, and an index. There is also a German translation: *Die Ordnung der Familie*, Frankfurt am Main, 1980

3. Michel Foucault, *La Volonte de Savoir*, Paris, 1976.

4. Philippe Ariès, *L'Enfant et la vie familiale sous l'ancien régime*, Paris: 1960; English translation: *Centuries of Childhood: A Social History of Family Life*, New York: 1962;

Peter Laslett, *The World We Have Lost*, London: 1965;

Edward Shorter, *The Making of the Modern Family*, Glasgow: 1975;

Eli Zaretsky, *Capitalism, the Family and Personal Life*, London: 1976.

5. For an explanation of Donzelot's theoretical starting points see Chapter 1 (American edition) and forewords by Donzelot and Deleuze.

6. This would not be true, for Zaretsky, but nowhere is it apparent that Donzelot knows Zaretsky's book. In general he is careless in naming his sources.

7. Donzelot, *Policing of Families*, p. 8.

8. Lasch, on the cover of the American edition of Donzelot, *Policing of Families*.

9. Donzelot, *Policing of Families*, XXII.

10. Yes this is what he says. Donzelot is inclined to portray the state or psychoanalysis as things which can think.

11. Donzelot, *Policing of Families*, p. XVI.

12. We refer English readers for summaries to Paul Hirst, note 13; Jill Hodges and Athar Hussain, *La Polices des Familles* (review)

in: *Ideology and Consciousness*, Spring, 1979, no. 5.

13. The expression 'History from a male standpoint' is used by Fran Bannett, Bea Campbell, Rosalind Coward in their reply to a very good review of Donzelot by Paul Hirst. See Paul Hirst, 'The Genesis of the Social' and Bennett *et al.*, 'Feminists, the Degenerates of the Social?' in *Politics and Power, no. 3, 'Sexual Politics, Feminism and Socialism'*, London: 1981, pp. 67–95.

14. Gayle Rubin, 'The Traffic in Women: Notes on the "Political Economy of Sex"' in: Rayna R. Reiter (ed.), *Towards an Anthropology of Women'*, New York and London: 1975.

15. See for example Linda Gordon, *Woman's Body, Woman's Right. A Social History of Birth Control in America*, London: 1977.

16. Barbara Ehrenreich, Deirdre English, *For Her Own Good*, New York: 1978 and London: 1979.

17. Donzelot, *Policing of Families*, p. 58.

18. Donzelot, *ibid*, p. XXXIII.

19. Donzelot, *ibid*, p. 91.

20. Renee Römkens, 'Resistance by battered women, a matter of power and impotence' in: *Tijdschrift voor Vrouwenstudies*, 1980, no. 3. p. 292.

21. In her description of the ideology on women in the 1950s, Elisabeth Wilson makes this point. 'Housekeeping as a career' might imply recognition of the importance and heaviness of the work that housewives do, but the ideology of 'also important in their own field' means that the status of women is heightened within the field at home, which is traditionally that of the housewife and socially of less value. It is therefore not a real change in the power relations between men and women. See Elisabeth Wilson, *Only Halfway to Paradise, Women in Postwar Britain: 1945–1968*, London: 1980.

22. Dorothy Dinnerstein, *The Mermaid and the Minotaur: Sexual Arrangements and Human Malaise*, New York: 1976;

Adrienne Rich, *Of Woman Born. Motherhood as Experience and Institution*, New York: 1976;

Nancy Chodorow, *The Reproduction of Mothering. Pschoanalysis and the Sociology of Gender*, Berkeley, Los Angeles and London: 1978.

Donzelot should have read Simone de Beauvoir *La Deuxieme sexe*

I: Les faits et les mythes, Paris: 1949: 'The woman is feared as a mother, therefore she must be adored and subjugated in motherhood'.

23. For a more extensive examination of the relationship between female power in private and public spheres see: Margaret Stacey and Marion Price, *Women Power and Politics*, London and New York, 1981.

24. See Veronica Beechy 'On Patriarchy' in: *Feminist Review*, 1979, no. 3. pp. 66–83.

25. Jalna Hanmer, 'Violence and the Social Control of Women', in: G.B. Smart Littlejohn, J. Wakeford and M. Yuval-Davis (eds.), *Power and the State*, London, 1978.

26. Selma Sevenhuijsen, 'Vadertje Staat, moedertje Thuis', in: *Socialisties-Feministiese Teksten*, Amsterdam, 1978.

27. See: Rachel Harrison, Frank Mort, 'Patriarchal Aspects of Nineteenth-Century State Formation: Property Relations, Marriage and Divorce, and Sexuality' in: Philip Corrigan, *Capitalism, State Formation and Marxist Theory, Historical Investigations*, London, 1980, pp. 79–111.

28. Julia Brophy and Carol Smart: 'From Disregard to Disrepute: The Position of Women in Family Law' in: *Feminist Review*, Vol 9 Autumn 1981.

29. Brophy and Smart, *ibid*

30. See Ehrenreich and English, *For Her Own Good*, chapters 6 and 7.

31. Donzelot, *Policing of Families*, p. 158.

32. Donzelot, *ibid*, p. 139.

33. See Annick Verbraken, 'Wordt Vaders wil wet? Ontwikkelingen in het Omgangsrecht' in: *Socialisties-Feministiese Teksten 6*, Amsterdam, 1981.

34. Donzelot, *The Policing of Families*, p. 36.

35. Kathleen Barry, *Female Sexual Slavery*, Englewood Cliffs, New Jersey, 1979, pp. 14–38.

36. Barry, *ibid*, p. 24.

37. Frits van Wel in: *Te Elfder Ure* 27, 'Sexualiteit', Nijmegen: 1980, p. 48. An extensive critique of his article, 'De Feminisering van de sexualiteit' appeared previously in: *Tijdschrift voor Vrouwenstudies*, 1981, no. 3 (M. Brügmann, M. Geurtsen, A.

Hoogenboom, A. Komter, S. Lammers, R. van Og, J. Withuis).
38. Hans Achterhuis, *De Markt van Welzijn en Geluk. Een kritiek van de andragogie*, Baarn: pp. 211–214 and 244–247.
39. Christopher Lasch, *Haven in a Heartless World, The Familiy Besieged*, New York, 1979. See also Lasch's review of Donzelot: 'Life in the Therapeutic State' in: *New York Review of Books*, 12, June 1980.
40. Originally, 'narcissistic' was an expression from clinical psychoanalysis. It is used by Lasch to describe a type of personality often seen nowadays and characterized, among other things, by: over-preoccupation with oneself, leading, for example, to hypochondria, inability to sustain relationships with others and to experience feelings, a perpetual search for insatiable superficial beauty, lack of conscience. We shall not elaborate here on the problems of transplanting clinical concepts to social theories or on the criticism levelled at Lasch concerning the degree in which such personalities actually occur.
41. 'Permissiveness' concerns the general atmosphere, said to be found mostly in families and schools where 'everything is allowed'.
42. In functionalistic arguments all events, developments, agencies etc. are seen as part (namely a function) of a system regarded as an organic whole.

6. Women's struggles in the Third World

1. It is not surprising that Surinamers seek safety in large numbers in the Netherlands as tensions increase in their own country.
2. See Klitorektomie, het recht op onze eigen sexualiteit, Amsterdam, Dolle Mina, 1976.
3. A. G. Frank, 'Ontwikkeling van de onderontwikkeling' in *Te Elfder Ure* no. 3/4, Nijmegen: SUN, 1969, p. 151.
4. See S. Amin, *et al.*, *Imperialisme en onderontwikkeling*, Nijmegen: SUN, 1976, p. 51.
5. E. Galeano, *De aderlating van een kontinent*, Amsterdam: Kritiese Bibliotheek Van Gennep, 1974, p. 9.
6. Meillassoux was one of the first to emphasize the interest of control over reproductive relations in precapitalist societies in C. Meillassoux, *Femmes, Greniers et Capitaux*, Paris: Maspero, 1975.

See for a feminist critique of his concept of reproduction: Felicity Edholm, Olivia Harris, Kate Young, 'Conceptualizing women' in *Critique of Anthropology*, nos. 9 and 10, vol. 3, 1977, pp. 101–31. See also Lucy Bland, Rachel Harrison, Frank Mort, Christine Weedon, 'Relations of reproduction: approaches through anthropology' in *Women's Studies Group, Women Take Issue*, London: Hutchinson, 1978, pp. 155–76.

7. There is no process of unambiguous class-forming in Third World countries. Elements of different modes of production from communal to monopoly capitalist overlap. Therefore, we cannot simply speak of classes.

8. In the film *Double Day*, statements by a white Latin American woman on a luxury yacht about the motives of women on her continent for going out to work display total inability to understand.

9. Seminar on the role of women in integrated rural development with emphasis on population problems, FAO report, UN, Cairo, 1974.

10. Heidi Hartmann goes into this in her article 'Kapitalisme, patriarchaat en de dubbele arbeidsmarkt', in *Socialisties-Feministiese Teksten* 2, Amsterdam: Feministische Uitgeverij Sara, 1978, pp. 41–9.

11. Galeano, *op. cit.*, p. 9.

12. Prostitution is a widespread phenomenon in Africa. For Latin America the International Labour Organization (ILO) gives the following, conservative figures: in Caracas, Venezuela: 80,000 prostitutes, of whom 27,000 do not receive medical treatment. In Sao Paulo, Brazil: 100,000 prostitutes, i.e. one per hundred inhabitants. (Data from: Margaret Randall, *You Can't Make a Revolution Without Them*, Toronto: 1975).

13. Sheila Rowbotham, *Women, Resistance and Revolution*, London: Penguin, 1972, p. 212.

14. In the west too there are differences between the aims of the women's movement and population policy. See Anna Davin, 'Imperialism and motherhood' in *History Workshop*, 5, Spring 1978, pp. 9–69 and Linda Gordon's article elsewhere in the collection.

15. See Bonnie Mass, *Population Target*, Toronto: Latin America

Working Group, 1976 and various articles in *ISIS* 7, *Vrouwen en Gezondheid*, Pt I, Carouge/Geneva, Rome, Dordrecht: 1978.

16. Galeano, *op. cit.*, pp. 15–16.

17. Linda Gordon, *Women's Body, Women's Right*, London: Penguin, 1977, p. 402.

18. Davin, *op. cit.*

19. F. Fröbel, J. Heinrichs, O. Kreye, 'Export-oriented industrialization of underdeveloped countries' in *Monthly Review*, 30, November 1978, pp. 22–8. These authors examine the new international division of labour in great detail, and point out the role of women in it as a cheap interchangeable labour force.

20. A more extensive critique is supplied by the Vrouwengroep Anthropologie Amsterdam in their article 'Vrouwen en werk in de Derde Wereld' in *Wetenschap en Samenleving* 79/2, March 1979, pp. 17–25.

21. PAIGC stands for African Party for the Independence of Guinea Bissau and the Cape Verde Islands.

22. Samora Machel, 'De bevrijding van de vrouw is een noodzakelijke voorwaarde voor de revolutie' in *Mozambique, revolutie in praktijk*, Amsterdam: Mondlane Stichting, 1974.

23. Martha Ford in discussion with Domitila, Support Group for International Women's Solidarity on 3 April 1979 in Amsterdam.

24. Domitila Chungara, Bolivian miner's wife and housewife, in Moena Vizier, *Mag ik zo vrij zijn* (Ghent: Kritak, 1978) tells how she disagreed with American feminists at the congress in Mexico during the International Women's Year in 1975. Her disapproving view of western feminism is one of the few written examples of such criticism from the Third World. Her view was eagerly seized on by the western press to suggest that women's problems only sprang from luxury.

25. The family in Third World countries cannot be equated with the family here. Families are often part of a larger living community. Families are not closed off from one another.

26. OMM is the abbreviation of Organization of Mozambique Women.

27. FMC is the abbreviation of Federation of Cuban Women.

28. Examples of this can be found in P. Caplan and J. Bujra (eds), *Women United, Women Divided: Cross Cultural Perspectives on*

Female Solidarity, London: Tavistock, 1978.

29. Some Dutch publications on women's struggle in the Third World are: *Oman, Socialisme zonder Sluier*, Amsterdam: Werkgroep Vrouwen en de Derde Wereld in samenwerking with het Palestina Committee, 1976. *Vrouwen in Chili*, Nijmegen: Latijns Amerika Vrouwengroep, 1978. Vrouwengroep Venceremos, *Cubaanse Vrouwen aan het Woord*, Cubareeks 3, Utrecht: USP, 1977. Anti-Apartheidsbeweging Nederland, *Vrouwenstrijd in Zuidelijk Afrika*, Amsterdam: AABN, 1978. Organisatie van Surinaamse Vrouwen, *Vrouw zijn in Suriname*, Amsterdam: Dokumentatie Centrum over de Vrouw, OSV, 1976.

30. NCO is the National Commission on Information and Consciousness-raising for Development Cooperation.